Leadership Communication:

A Scriptural Perspective

Leadership Communication:

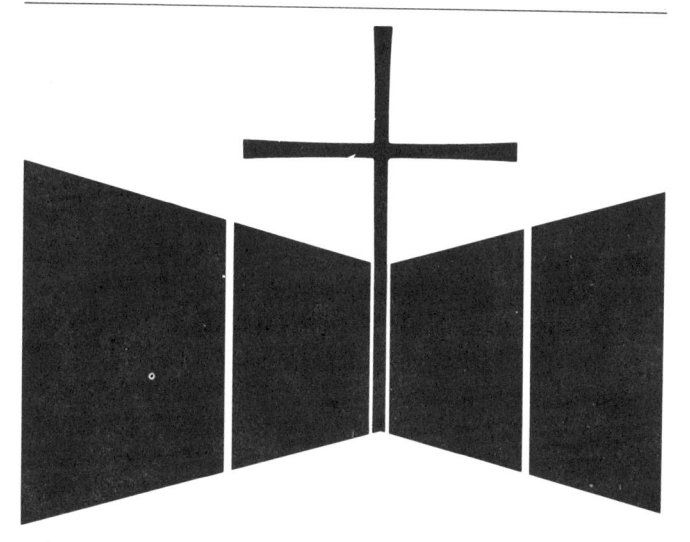

A Scriptural Perspective

Richard L. Stoppe

LIBRARY OF CONGRESS
CATALOG CARD NUMBER: 82-62112

ISBN: 0-87148-519-2

First Printing: 10,000 November, 1982

Copyright © 1982 Church of God
Department of General Education

Unless otherwise specified, scriptural quotations were taken from the Revised Standard Version (New York: Thomas Nelson and Sons, 1952) except in those cases in which this writer made his own translations based on Nestle's Greek text or Kittel's Hebrew Text.

DEDICATION

Affectionately dedicated to my parents, the Reverend and Mrs. Henry C. Stoppe, now retired from an illustrious ministry; to my wife, Carolyn, and my children: Deborah, Richard Jr., Donald, Alan, and Douglas.

TABLE OF CONTENTS

	Foreword	9
	Preface	11
1	The Element of Persuasion	13
2	The Element of Trust	59
3	The Element of Love	91
4	The Element of Provisionalism	123
5	Empathic Understanding	149
6	Possibility Thinking	181
7	Problem-Solving	193
8	Leadership Principles	209
9	Power and Motivation	235

FOREWORD

Proper communication is considered by many to be the most vital element in a positive relationship. The Scripture has much to say about how we are to talk with one another. The basic information that we communicate to those to whom we minister is the key factor in the success of that relationship. A lack of proper information is at the heart of all personal, social and spiritual problems. The Lord declared this through the prophet Hosea: "My people are destroyed for lack of knowledge" (4:6).

Dr Richard Stoppe has done a great service to Christian leaders in writing *Leadership Communication: A Scriptural Perspective*. From a rich personal and professional background he adeptly articulates scriptural principles for the communicating of God's truths to meet human needs. By integrating psychological and theological concepts he gives the reader practical, yet biblically based, insights to successful communication.

The son of a Church of God minister, Dr. Stoppe is well qualified to write such a book as this. He currently serves as Professor of Organizational Behavior and Communication as well as Director of External Programs at Southern Illinois University. He is president of Consultant Specialists and is listed in *Con-*

sultants' Who's Who International. As a communication expert, he has conducted over 300 seminars for businesses and service organizations and has given ministerial seminars in over 60 denominations. His academic credits include the B.A. from Upsala College, the M.A. from Wheaton College and the Ph.D. from Wayne State University.

Leadership Communication is a unique book. The author has brought a Christian perspective, a technical skill and an interesting writing style to an area of study which too often is approached from one of two extremes: a shallow, popular treatment or a tedious, technical point of view. This uniqueness, coupled with the need to which it speaks, makes this book an especially effective tool for Christian leaders at all levels.

Robert E. Fisher, Ph.D.

PREFACE

Approximately 75 percent of a leader's working time is spent communicating, and 75 percent of that time is spent in oral, face-to-face communication. Therefore, *Leadership Communication* is worth studying in depth.

Jesus lamented that, "The sons of this age are wiser in their own generation than the sons of light" (Luke 16:8). Never before has it been so imperative for those communicating the greatest message to keep pace with contemporary knowledge as it relates to scriptural truth.

The analysis and suggestions in *Leadership Communication* are based on hundreds of communicative studies. This book is also based on the principles of Scripture. Truth in whatever discipline it is found is always in harmony with God, because "the Spirit is the truth" (1 John 5:7).

Unless otherwise specified, scriptural quotations were taken from the Revised Standard Version (New York: Thomas Nelson and Sons, 1952) except in those cases in which this writer made his own translations based on Nestle's Greek text or Kittel's Hebrew text.

My thanks to the members of the Church of God Department of General Education, and especially to Dr. Robert Fisher for invaluable assistance.

Richard L. Stoppe, Ph.D.
St. Louis, Missouri

1

THE ELEMENT OF PERSUASION

Christian pastors deserve high commendation. Their task is one of the world's most difficult. Their competition, for example, is almost unparalleled. On Saturday night a popular evangelist has a horse on stage. He asks the stallion, "Do you love Jesus?" The horse neighs and nods to the delight of youngsters and adults alike. The same audience naively wonders, "Why does Sunday morning worship service at my church seem so dull?"

A minister approaches the first day of the week with a sermon burning in his heart. He is aware, however, that fourteen hours before his congregation will hear him, a Billy Graham special will be shown on television. All the contagious excitement of a football stadium packed to capacity, a famous quarterback giving his testimony, and a 5,000-voice choir singing "How Great Thou Art" appear to dwarf the pastor's efforts by comparison.

A couple of hours before the pastor is to speak, an Oral Roberts television special reaches his congregation. This time the World Action Singers display their talents in chorale and choreography aboard an Alaskan harbor ferry against the backdrop of azure water and snowcapped mountains. Moments before, Oral Roberts has alighted from a helicopter onto a glacier of Mount McKinley, the highest peak in North America, and discussed his faith from the height of 20,000 feet. Viewers wonder why suddenly the pulpit at their church seems so low.

This chapter is designed to help Christian leaders understand the dynamics of persuasive communication. Hopefully, it will assist all Christians in communicating the greatest message of all by integrating and identifying the gospel with needs of men and women, young and old.

Through the years many books have been written on the life of Christ. The authors, while often giving valuable insights, have usually so highly colored Christ's portrait by majoring on or distorting some particular aspect of His life teaching, that the books have been more revealing of the authors than of Jesus. Thus, Ernest Renan presents Jesus as a weak sentimentalist. Bouck White sees Him as a social revolutionary, destroying the customs and traditions of the past. Bruce Barton describes Jesus as a supersalesman whose skills and strategy would thrill the heart of a modern vice-president of sales and marketing. Albert Schweitzer and Maurice Goguel see Jesus as an apocalyptic figure, expecting the end of the world in His generation. Thomas Carver would give Jesus a Ph.D. in economics while Middleton Murry would grant Him a Ph.D. in education, seeing Him as a teacher of genius. Joseph Klausner, a Jewish scholar, discovers an unorthodox Galilean rabbi. T. R. Glover thinks he explains Jesus when he describes the dynamics of His personality. Rudolph Bultmann demythologizes Jesus into a dynamic preacher. And Harry Emerson Fosdick dwarfs Jesus into a human artistic genius as he views Him through the eyes of His contemporaries.

No attempt in this book will be made to present Christ as a communicational psychologist. Yet an examination of His message will demonstrate His understanding of persuasive communication. By His words and actions, Jesus observed a cardinal rule of effective communication: You persuade a person only to the extent that you come into his world of experience, speak his language, and identify your message with his needs, motives, and desires.

We tend to see things not as they are but as we are. We see what we are conditioned to see. We see with our experience, our emotions, our aspirations, and our expectations. We see with our feelings as well as our eyes.

At the end of a semester, I asked a group of university teachers to identify five of the students they liked best and five they liked least from any class. The graded papers of these students were then examined carefully. It was discovered that these professors missed approximately 33 percent more mistakes by the students they liked than by the ones they disliked. Yet each instructor was quite confident before the experiment that he had treated all students equally regarding such errors. An even more astonishing bias came to light with college sophomores rating one another in a separate but related experiment. Students in the study overlooked twice as many mistakes from the papers of peers well liked!

Here is a little example to show how we can be conditioned visually and audibly. Suppose I write the symbols . . .

A13C

on the chalkboard and ask a student to read these "letters." He reads them as the first three letters of the alphabet. Then I erase the **A** and **C** only, substituting **12** and **14** respectively . . .

12 13 14

I ask a late-arriving student to read these "numbers." The middle symbol becomes a letter or a number depending upon the conditioning.

This selective process of decoding meaning is a common psychological phenomenon familiar to all of us. In the above example we are conditioned by our past experience with numerical and alphabetical symbols. In a similar manner, we are always preconditioned by our needs, goals, and desires. With keen insight Mahatma Gandhi contemplated the plight of India's famished millions: "Even God, if He wanted to speak to a starving man, would have to speak in terms of bread." The story of the Incarnation is a beautiful example of God communicating to man in human language and experience.

All classifications of human needs and goals are somewhat arbitrary. Varying lists abound. The following categorization developed by the late Abraham Maslow is the most widely used classification today in the texts of advertising, marketing, personnel administration, sales management, and interpersonal or persuasive communication.[1] In order of their dominance, the five needs that shape our thought, action, and response are . . .

1. The physiological needs of survival and preservation
2. The needs of security and safety
3. The needs of loving, being loved, and belonging
4. The needs of esteem
5. The needs of adventure, self-actualization, and fulfillment.

APPEALING TO PHYSIOLOGICAL NEEDS

Our strongest needs are physical. The primary needs of survival and preservation are oxygen, food, water, rest, exercise, shelter, excretion, and sex.

Jesus often expressed His message in terms of physical needs. What was the overriding physical need of the people of Palestine in A. D. 29? Was it not nourishment to assuage their hunger, and rest for their tired, overworked bodies?

You will recall that the first request in the Lord's Prayer is bread; the second, forgiveness (Matthew 6:11; Luke 11:3). The order is not coincidental. The order is

---

[1] A. H. Maslow, *Motivation and Personality*, 2nd ed. (New York: Harper and Row, 1970). See also A. H. Maslow, "A Theory of Human Motivation," *Psychological Review*, L (1943), 370-96.

deliberate and meaningful. It is only in some relationship to a need that the gospel message becomes personally relevant.

Again, hear Christ speaking to the multitude: "Blessed are you that hunger now, for you shall be satisfied" (Luke 6:21). In the verse before, Christ called the poor blessed. Jesus reached His audience when poverty and hunger could be equated with good fortune! To peasants on the bottom of the social register, looked down upon by their religious leaders, Jesus was identifying with their needs.

Keep in mind the penury of Christ's audience. Perhaps our Lord was speaking about spiritual food, but notice the identification as He spoke of the commodity that meant most to His listeners: "I am the bread." Twelve times it is recorded that Christ called Himself bread (John 6:32, 33, 34, 35, 41, 48, 50, 51, 58).

Before an audience of 5,000 men, besides women and children, Jesus borrowed five barley loaves and two fish from a lad. Then He multiplied the loaf to feed them all until they were completely satisfied. Twelve basketsful were left over. Then Jesus withdrew to the hills because the multitude tried to "take him by force to make him king" (John 6:15). Here was a Man who could provide food. "He who comes to me," Jesus said, "shall not hunger" (John 6:35).

What about the need for rest? Observe the invitational call you have often savored: "Come to me, all who labor and are heavy laden, and I will give you rest. . . . My yoke is easy, and my burden is light" (Matthew 11:28). For men working from sunrise to sunset six days a week, in a culture where the employer was everything and the employee was nothing, Jesus may have meant spiritual rest, but His hearers integrated His message with the thought of physical rest.

Recall with me the story of Christ and the woman of Samaria. There being no running water or even a hand pump for a cistern or well, the heroine in our story trudged perhaps three-quarters of a mile with a pot on her head to fetch water from the town well. Jesus realized that to succeed with any spiritual message He first had to speak in terms of her need—in this case, water. "Every one who drinks of this water will thirst again, but whoever drinks of the water that I shall give him will never thirst." Is it not obvious that the woman perceived Christ's words in a literal, physical sense when she replied: "Sir, give me this water, that I may not thirst, nor come here to draw" (John 4:13-15)?

Consider these words of Jesus and their obvious impact: "Do not be anxious about your life, what you shall eat or what you shall drink, nor about your body, what you shall put on. . . . Look at the birds of the air: they neither sow nor reap nor gather into barns, yet your heavenly Father feeds them. Are you not of more value than they? . . . And why are you anxious about clothing? Consider the lilies of the field, how they grow; they neither toil nor spin; yet I tell you, even Solomon in all his glory was not arrayed like one of these. But if God so clothes the grass of the field, which today is alive and tomorrow is thrown into the oven, will he not much more clothe you?" (Matthew 6:25-30).

One of the oldest Gospel fragments ever discovered —a parchment found in Egypt from the Ruins of

Oxyrhynchus, dated before A. D. 150—reads: "He [God] himself will give you your garment."[2] "Therefore do not be anxious saying, 'What shall we eat?' or 'What shall we drink?' or 'What shall we wear?' For . . . your heavenly Father knows that you need them all" (Matthew 6:31, 32).

Here was a direct appeal to the physical needs of food, drink, shelter, and apparel. Jesus' listeners felt the pangs of these needs, so He spoke to these needs. Finally, however, Christ tied the physical and spiritual together as the sermon continued: "But seek first his kingdom and his righteousness, and all these things shall be yours as well" (Matthew 6:33).

King David reminisced in old age: "I have not seen the righteous forsaken or his children begging bread" (Psalm 37:25). Jesus reaffirmed divine providence under the New Covenant: "Ask, and it will be given you; seek, and you will find; knock, and it will be opened to you. For every one who asks receives, and he who seeks finds, and to him who knocks it will be opened. Or what man of you, if his son asks him for bread, will give him a stone? Or if he asks for a fish, will give him a serpent? If you then, who are evil, know how to give good gifts to your children, how much more will your Father who is in heaven give good things to those who ask him!" (Matthew 7:7-11).

Former ambassador to Russia, George F. Kennan, says in his memoirs: "One of the things I have had to learn in life is that in political matters truth prematurely uttered is of scarcely greater value than error."[3] What a lesson for aspiring political ambassa-

---

[2] *Oxyrhynchus Papyri,* Part LV, 1904, vs. 15.
[3] *Memoirs: 1950-1963* (Atlantic, Little, Brown), *Reader's Digest,* March, 1976, p. 73.

dors! What a lesson for aspiring Christian ambassadors as well!

First determine the need. Then relate your message to that need. Truth uttered prematurely could be a serious liability. The physiological being the greatest need of His hearers, Christ frequently identified His message with that need.

While the physical needs were the most important for Christ's audience, they are not the most important for ours. Advertising studies indicate that here in the contiguous United States we are at any given time 85 percent satisfied physiologically. For this reason, this strongest and most basic need becomes the weakest. This would not be true in many other countries of the world. One ministering to the poor of South India could not ignore the advice of Mahatma Gandhi given early in this century; one would still have to speak in terms of bread. But for the overwhelming majority here in the United States, we have the means to satisfy our physiological needs. Even our poor are rich by comparison with the mendicant of Third World nations, where welfare, unemployment benefits, food stamps, Medicare, Aid to Families With Dependent Children (AFDC), and the like do not exist.

This does not mean that we should ignore the physiological needs of the United States. Any given family can feel the pinch of unemployment and experience the embarrassment of Mother Hubbard's cupboard. Few are immune to galloping inflation, especially those on fixed incomes. It does mean, however, that by and large in our culture, we can expect a higher degree of responsiveness by identifying the greatest message with other needs.

APPEALING TO SECURITY NEEDS

The secondmost dominant need of man is that of security. In the United States, appeals to this need are more rewarding than appeals to physical needs because, as we have seen, most are able to satisfy the basics.

We are concerned about our families if we should die, so we purchase life insurance. Concerned about the expense of prolonged illness, we participate in a health plan at work or purchase hospitalization insurance. We visualize with Solomon "the day when the keepers of the house tremble, and the strong men are bent, and the grinders . . . are few, and those that look through the windows are dimmed" (Ecclesiastes 12:3). So we select a retirement plan or depend upon Social Security to protect ourselves from want "before the silver cord is snapped, or the golden bowl is broken . . . and the spirit returns to God who gave it" (Ecclesiastes 12:6, 7). Some of us have disability insurance to ensure that our salaries will continue if catastrophe should strike. Job seniority or tenure, union contract grievance procedures, unemployment benefits, and cost-of-living clauses have greatly appeased our longing for security. Many accept a job that offers security first and high wages second.

Obviously, insurance companies thrive on this need. I still vividly recall a visit from a life insurance agent when I bought my first house. A video-tape screen showed a father playing basketball with his 12-year-old son in the driveway of their home. An accompanying record spoke of the wonderful relationship between the two. Suddenly an **X** crossed out the father; the record played a funeral threnody; a coffin was lowered into the ground; and I was asked, "What will happen to the boy now? Will his college plans still materialize?" A "for sale" sign appeared on the house. The screen went dark, the record stopped, and I was asked to sign on the dotted line.

In Christ's time, a man anxious about the perils of prolonged illness could not purchase Blue Cross or Blue Shield. Nor was workman's compensation provided in case of injury. Everywhere exorcists, charlatans, and magic pools exacerbated disappointment (John 5:7). Metropolitan Life Insurance agents had no offices in Chorazin, Bethsaida, or Capernaum, or in any of the other towns visited by Christ. Nor had Prudential yet discovered the Rock of Gibraltar. The pioneer work of Samuel Gompers (1850-1924), the father of the modern labor movement, was nearly two millennia in the future. Roman soldiers were constant reminders of political subjection and curtailed civil liberties. In such a climate, Jesus came offering the security of divine care: "Your Father knows what you need before you ask him" (Matthew 6:8).

Much has been written about Christ's prophecy concerning the near future—that He would "come with his angels in the glory of the Father" to bring judgment upon every man; that there would be those standing in his audience who would "not taste death before" they would see Him "coming in his kingdom" (Matthew 16:27-28; 24:29-34; Mark 13:24-30; Luke 21:25-32). Much has been written about Paul's expectation of Christ's return during his lifetime (1 Corinthians 15:51), and much has been written about the church in Jerusalem finding it reasonable for its members to sell their property (Acts 4:32-35). Albert Schweitzer, Maurice Goguel, and their followers mistakingly assume that

Christ was concerned with the imminent future rather than the present.[4]

However, Jesus also spoke about exorbitant rents charged poor people for residency in hovels. He spoke about the usury of loan sharks. He condemned corrupt courts that were partial to the rich men. He mocked a caste system that would permit a starving man to die at the gate of the prosperous. When Jesus preached about such matters, He was certainly speaking to the security needs of His listeners in the present (Matthew 18:28-30; 5:20; Luke 16:20-22).

The Bible has much to say about security. It speaks clearly to man's secondmost potent need. The beautiful concept of justification by faith is one of the greatest messages of security we could ever preach. In reaction against unconditional election and eternal security, some branches of the body of Christ have been guilty of preaching insecurity. Let us affirm, whether we are in the Calvinistic or Arminian tradition, that we do not stand in our own righteousness. We are clothed with the righteousness of Christ. This is an imputed righteousness, the Bible says. God does not look at us with all our failures and shortcomings. "If thou, Lord, shouldest mark iniquities, O Lord, who shall stand?" asked the Psalmist, "But there is forgiveness with thee . . ." (Psalm 130:3, 4, KJV).

Jesus taught Christians to pray: "Forgive us our sins" (Luke 11:4). The Apostle Paul explained: "All have sinned and *fall short* of the glory of God" (Romans 3:23). The second verb is present, indicative, middle

---

[4] See, for example, Albert Schweitzer's *The Quest for the Historical Jesus* and Maurice Goguel's *The Life of Jesus*.

voice in Greek, *husterountai*, and denotes continuing action. He who claims that he does not fall short of the glory of God boasts not of superior holiness, but of superior blindness. The greatest of all sins is to be conscious of none. Fortunately, we do not stand in our own righteousness. "All our righteous deeds are like a polluted garment," the Bible says (Isaiah 64:6). Dressed in rags, "None is righteous, no, not one" (Romans 3:10). Unless we believe as the old-time Wesleyans, the day of perfection will elude us as long as we live. Yet Christ will present us spotless and blameless, because the Father looks on the Son's righteousness and not on ours.

Security is a vital need of men and women. You may appeal to this need through the words of Jesus: "My sheep hear my voice, and I know them, and they follow me; and I give them eternal life, and they shall never perish, and no one shall snatch them out of my hand" (John 10:27, 28). You may teach from the verse, "Who shall bring any charge against God's elect?" and answer with Paul, "It is God who justifies" (Romans 8:33). You may share with others the treasure, "Who is to condemn?" and reply, "[It is] Christ Jesus, who . . . is at the right hand of God, who indeed intercedes for us" (Romans 8:34). You may raise the question, "Who shall separate us from the love of Christ? Shall tribulation, or distress, or persecution, or famine, or nakedness, or peril, or sword?" and affirm, "I am sure that neither death, nor life, nor angels, nor principalities, nor things present, nor things to come, nor powers, nor height, nor depth, nor anything else in all creation, will be able to separate us from the love of God in Christ Jesus our Lord" (Romans 8:35, 38, 39).

The imagery of "Christ, the door," connotes a beautiful concept of security (John 10:9). When about six years of age, I frequently wondered what kind of door Christ was. Perhaps He was a house door, I thought, or maybe a church door. Then grasping some concept of antiquity, I suspected that Christ might be something like an old barn door. One day Dad took me to a big bank downtown and showed me where he kept his safety deposit box. We went through a large round door—you know, the kind with scores of knobs or latches on them. In my preadolescent framework I thought, "If Christ is any kind of a door, He must be a great strong door like that."

As I grew older, I considered the passage to be figurative until my early twenties when I visited Israel. There I saw shepherds tending sheep just as their forefathers had done in the time of Christ. At evening time one shepherd gently led his sheep into a mountainside cave, patting and counting every one while calling each by name. One by one the sheep jumped up over the ledge into safety. My big surprise and revelation came when the shepherd took out a blanket from his backpack and stretched it across the entrance. Then the shepherd put his head at one end and his feet at the other. The shepherd himself was the door! Let the animals of prey come. They must face the shepherd first. Spiritually, let "the accuser of [the] brethren" (Revelation 12:10) charge us with sin, he must face the righteousness of Christ first. Christ is the door.

God says, "Behold, I have graven you on the palms of my hands" (Isaiah 49:16). For years Sears has advertised that we "are in good hands with Allstate." How much more security we have, engraved in the palms of God! We are not just chalked or painted on God's hands. We are etched there as a sculptor engraves his name in granite. We are graven on His hands forever.

Particularly with senior citizens and especially with the terminally ill, the greatest need of security concerns the subject of death. The psychology of gerontology deals with, among other things, preparing older persons to face death. During Colonial times in America, the high incidence of disease made life expectancy only 35 years of age. Even 100 years ago, the average person could not expect to reach 40. By 1970, however, life expectancy climbed above 72. With an expanding senior population, psychologists, psychiatrists, and ministers are increasingly treating the problem of insecurity caused by the prospect of dying. Frankly, the non-Christian counselor has little to offer. Books like *Life Begins at Death*, void of Christian message, are also void of hope.

All life insurance policies are designed for the beneficiary, not the deceased. The Christian, however, bears witness to an exclusive life insurance policy. It is the only policy designed for the insured.

Richard Neibuhr, age 90, called me at 2:30 a.m. one morning to tell me that the end of his life was near. I was a young man, serving as student pastor, and had provided his ride to church each Sunday. Soon I was at his bedside reading from his favorite Bible passage, John 14: "In my Father's house are many rooms; if it were not so, would I have told you that I go to prepare a place for you? And when I go and prepare a place for you, I will come again and will take you to myself, that where I am you may be also."

Mr. Neibuhr stopped me right there and began to talk. "You know that sermon you gave last Sunday about Jesus turning the water into wine?"

I nodded affirmatively.

"The governor of the feast told the wedding host that, contrary to custom, he had saved the best wine for last. And remember how you said 'God always saves the best for last'?"

"I remember," I said.

"Well, I can testify," Neibuhr continued, "that serving God in my youth was wonderful, but every subsequent period of my life has been better. Truly, the Christian faith is 'sweeter as the years go by,' and 'every day with Jesus is sweeter than the day before' as the songwriters say." Squeezing my hand, he continued: "Richie [he always called me that], this past year under your ministry was the very best. Keep up the good work."

With those words he closed his eyes to answer the roll call of the Church Triumphant. But undoubtedly in the next few moments Neibuhr was exclaiming, "O God, You have saved the best for last!" For the Bible assures us that "[to] be away from the body [is to be] at home with the Lord" (2 Corinthians 5:8).

God always saves the best for last. "All that a man has he will give for his life," said Satan to God in the narrative of Job (2:4), probably as much a truism to the viewers of the modern play *J. B.* as to the first readers of the ancient scrolls.[5] Against death, the greatest fear of man in all ages, the Christian message

---

[5] *J. B.* is a modern play by H. C. Bunner based on the biblical narrative of Job.

makes its most prodigious claim. What security we can offer! When death has dug its last grave, and hewn its last tomb, Jesus will still stand on the golden hills of eternity and proclaim, "I am the resurrection and the life; he who believes in me, though he die, yet shall he live, and whosoever lives and believes in me shall never die" (John 11:25, 26). The Good Shepherd promises to lead His sheep safely not only along the mountainsides of this life, but also "through the valley of the shadow of death" (Psalm 23:4; John 10:27, 28; Luke 18:30).

Advertising studies show that in the United States 30 percent of the people are insecure at any given time. In periods of economic recession or for those in the autumn of life, this figure can rise significantly. Communicate the gospel in terms of security.

APPEALING TO LOVE NEEDS

The love need encompasses a cluster of needs including to love, to be loved, and to belong. Love is the thirdmost dominant need of man, if there is substantial lack of satisfaction in security and physiological needs. In our culture, appeals associated with love tend to be much more successful on the average than security and physiological appeals. At any given time people in the United States are 50 percent unsatisfied in the category of love.

This figure rises substantially for the teenager whose high school romance has just been shattered. Often parents and onlookers underestimate the importance of the breakup. To some, it was only puppy love or adolescent infatuation. But to the one pining and yearning, this loss equals anguish.

Of course, the 50-percent figure rises even more dramatically for the one languishing in the trauma of divorce. The divorced person is severely neglected in most churches and treated like a leper in many churches. Surprising to many, divorce is usually emotionally harder on the man than on the woman. A divorce, in terms of stress, is estimated to be equivalent to that of a Ph.D. program! Most large companies have a personnel policy that prohibits hiring a person for an executive position within one year of a divorce. One-half of all couples marrying today will be divorced within fifteen years, if the present trends continue. The church must respond to these needs and make a commitment of love and acceptance as never before.

A person finds satisfaction for love needs most generally through his immediate family and close friends, but the need extends beyond this perimeter. We yearn for approval and the affection of peers and colleagues. We crave the love and appreciation of our supervisors and subordinates.

The most significant aspect of this dynamic need is that its satisfaction involves both giving and receiving —a reciprocity of loving and being loved. Shakespeare, unsurpassed at describing human emotion, makes much ado about unrequited love. Generally, the more a person gives, the more that person has a need to receive. The higher one's level of anxiety, the more he needs friends. Studies show that misery loves not only company, but miserable company. We tend to seek out others with like anxieties. Firstborn and only children have stronger affiliative needs than do later-born, although all have such needs.[6]

Besides loving and being loved, the concept of belonging is woven inseparably into the fabric of this need. We all need to belong to someone, to some group, formal or informal. We need a psychological sphere, a social structure, a warm niche where we feel comfortable and accepted. To the extent that our church or organizations can provide this psychological identity through membership, project, causes, purpose, services, classes, and special-interest groups, it will be successful. Strong family ties are important also to meet the need of belonging. Approximately 95 percent of delinquent children come from broken homes. The weaker the integration of the family, the more likely the children will engage in deviant behavior.[7]

Jesus recognized the potency of this need by calling it the distinguishing mark of His followers: "By this all men will know that you are my disciples, if you have love for one another" (John 13:35). When asked which statutes were paramount, Jesus replied, "[To] love the Lord your God with all your heart" and "[to] love your neighbor as yourself. There is no other commandment greater than these" (Mark 12:29, 30). For Jesus, this love was to extend even to enemies (Matthew 5:44), and *neighbor* was broadened to include all contacts, in the didactic Parable of the Good Samaritan (Luke 10:30-37).

---

[6] Stanley Schachter, *The Psychology of Affiliation* (Stanford, Calif.: Stanford University Press, 1959), pp. 101-25.

[7] Leonard Broom and Phillip Selznick, *Sociology: A Text With Adapted Readings* (New York, 1957), p. 406.

In the Parable of the Prodigal Son, Jesus taught that God loved both the wayward and the upright child equally (Luke 15:11-31). In Old Testament literature, God was portrayed occasionally as Father of the nation, but never of the individual (Exodus 4:22). Jesus instituted a new identification of belonging in which each could address God as Father (Matthew 6:9, 14, 26).

Christ identified His message with love and, perhaps more by example than by teaching, demonstrated its magnetism. We can picture the followers of Christ nodding affirmatively when hearing, "As the Father has loved me, so have I loved you" (John 15:9). They experienced His love collectively, for so often we read: "He had compassion for them" (Matthew 9:36; 14:14; 15:32; *et al*). They experienced His love individually, for we read: "Now Jesus loved Martha and her sister and Lazarus" (John 11:5).

There is no more attractive church than the loving church. The pastor who has a love relationship with the flock is winsome. Members who genuinely love the pastor, each other, and outsiders exhibit an irresistible charm. Nothing can ever substitute for the directive of Christ: "This is my commandment, that you love one another as I have loved you" (John 15:12).

When we turn our thoughts to the gospel, what an incomparable message we have to proclaim for the love needs of man. By contrast, the airline that loves us, or the shaving cream that loves our face, has little to offer. Much of the misery of the world can be attributed to homesickness—homesickness for God. Psychologists such as Rollo May in books such as *Man's Search for Himself* or *Psychology and the Human Dilemma* speak of contemporary man as feeling a sense of orphanage, estrangement, or being lost. The diagnosis is superb. The suggested remedy is ephemeral. Only God can satisfy the yearning of the human heart. But remember, God shows His love to others primarily through us.

The gospel lends itself inexhaustibly to meeting this need. "God so loved the world . . ." (John 3:16). "See what love the Father has given us, that we should be called children of God" (1 John 3:1). The gospel is the message of God's love for us. Salvation is the response of our love to Him. For everyone frightened into the church through the preaching of hell, 10 can be won through the preaching of love. It is the kindness of God that leads to repentance, according to the Bible (Romans 2:4).

The average American moves once every three years. Every week there are new families in your community who are searching for belonging and group affiliation. If one of these families should visit your church, your responsibility has just begun. Churches with some type of buddy system are highly successful in converting visitors to members. A buddy system is one in which a family of similar economic status, interests, and age is assigned to the new family, to provide a social identity—invitations to the home, parties, and other functions, as well as church.

The Spanish Pentecostal churches of New York City have a fantastic success story. Their program includes an organized and costly effort to find housing and jobs for new Spanish-speaking persons moving to the metropolis. The pastor of the largest church there told me that they are experiencing an 80-percent return on their investment; that is, 8 out of 10 persons assisted find their identity and church home with the group that showed friendship and warmth in a time of social transition. And get this: more than half of the newcomers had been previously associated with traditional denominations.

James Russo was refused admission to the college fraternity of his choice. His friends belonged; he did not. On the outside of things, he was despondent. At this point in life his social world collapsed and love was his greatest need. It was at this time that I witnessed to him of Christ. The approach? I talked about belonging to something and Someone that really counted. Soon Jim was singing, "Now I belong to Jesus." Now he felt loved. Now he belonged.

Present the gospel in terms of love and commitment —in terms of belonging and acceptance, both through message and example. Not only does God have us on His hands, He also has us on His heart! At any given time we are 50 percent unsatisfied in this category. Christians who communicate love will find responsive hearts.

APPEALING TO ESTEEM NEEDS

When our physiological, security, and love needs are relatively satisfied, our esteem needs become most important. In our culture, we are likely to be only 40 percent satisfied in this category. These other needs having been met substantially, Americans are particularly vulnerable to a persuasive arsenal aimed here.

Esteem needs may be divided into two principal types: first, how a person sees himself; second, how he thinks others see him.

To a large extent, our self-image determines, as well as reflects, the state of our mental health. A study was made of persons who came for psychological counseling. It was discovered that there was zero correlation between what the average patient thought of himself and what he believed an ideal person to be. The study confirmed that generally we are mentally healthy when we think well of ourselves and generally neurotic when we do not.[8] Our needs for self-esteem cause us to desire and seek strength, achievement, adequacy, mastery, and competence. We long for confidence in the face of difficulty, for independence, and for freedom.

As one might expect, studies tend to show that Americans are among the most achievement-oriented peoples of the world. The years from 8 to 10 are the most critical in determining the achievement motivation of a child. If the parents (especially the mother) expect the child during these years to know his way around town, to strive diligently for desired things, to take responsibility, to make his own friends, to do well in competition, to meet standards, and to make some important decisions—if the parents expect these things, the child probably will be achievement-oriented the rest of his life. Thereafter, the person will usually regard achievement as an end in itself. He will constantly seek feedback as to how he is performing and progressing. He will be persistently goal-oriented.[9]

---

[8] J. M. Butler and G. V. Haigh, *Changes in the Relation Between Self-concepts and Ideal Concepts Consequent Upon Client-centered Counseling.* C. R. Rogers and Rosalind F. Dymond, eds. *Psychotherapy and Personality Changes* (Chicago: University of Chicago Press, 1954), pp. 55-76. The correlation between the control group was .58. The exception is the psychotic patient, such as the schizophrenic, who distorts reality significantly enough to be happy with his assumed identity.

[9] David C. McClelland, *The Achieving Society*, ed. Van Nostrand Reinhold (New York: The Free Press, 1967), especially pp. 43-47; 340-41.

The achievement-oriented individual has lower affiliation needs than others. He needs only a few select friends and prefers to work with them if group action becomes necessary to reach a goal. He will respond to admonition to "try harder," to competition, and to a challenge to meet some standard of excellence.[10] If the achievement-oriented individual does not find in your church or organization the opportunity to do his best, to be successful, to accomplish tasks requiring skill and effort, to accomplish something important, to do a difficult task well—he will eventually take his talents elsewhere.

Competence and confidence are vital to the self-image. Feelings of inferiority and incompetence may lead to inertia, withdrawal, or refusal to participate in church activities for some people. For others, it may lead to frustration, aggression, negativism, and hostility. When the ego is bruised, it sometimes strikes with the venom of a cobra. What pastor or Sunday school superintendent has not experienced this at times? We need always to feel adequate for the demands of our social milieu and working environment.[11]

Independence and freedom are likewise essential. Mother and Father learn quickly that their little darlings can become tyrants chafing at parental reins. Adults as well as children resist favors with strings and gifts with bondage. We prefer helpful direction and rebel against rigid control. Freedom to perform a task with a minimum of supervision, allowing for a maximum of creativity, enhances the self-image.

---

[10] *Ibid.*

[11] For a full study of competence, see Robert W. White's *Lives in Progress* (New York: Holt, Reinhart, and Winston, 1966).

Any appeal, action, opportunity, or assignment that makes a person feel better about himself gives more reinforcement and makes him feel more of a man. Anything that inspires confidence, adequacy, and personal freedom will be psychologically motivating to the one with high esteem needs.

It is important that a person is not thrown into deep water before being taught to swim. Nothing is more detrimental to motivation than failure. Nothing is more reinforcing than repeated success. Utilize training courses, sponsor seminars, send key individuals to professional meetings, and provide an adequate library to develop the personnel resources of your church or organization. Train a person in the shallow end of the pool before jettisoning him into the deep end. Provide the opportunity for low diving, then high diving as the individual develops. Appoint a man as acting director before asking him to serve as a permanent director, depending on his past or comparable experience.

Here, all the sermons of the Norman Vincent Peale and Robert Schuller type—the message of a positive mental attitude—are rewarding. The principles of *Think and Grow Rich* by Napoleon Hill apply to spiritual wealth as well as material mammon. "I can do all things in him who strengthens me" and "We are more than conquerors through him who loved us" wrote Paul (Philippians 4:13; Romans 8:37). If someone has a problem, tell him, "That's good." Why is it good? It is good because repeated victories over problems are rungs on the ladder of success. Each victory brings growth and confidence. "Turn your scars into stars!" "If life gives you lemons, make lemonade."

People, unlike pottery, can become stronger when broken.

So someone doesn't feel like much. Quote the title and theme of Jess Lair's book *I Ain't Much, Baby—But I'm All I've Got.*[12] So someone has failed. So did Peter. After three years of training under the ministry of Jesus, he denied he ever knew Him! Remember the philosophy of Ralph Waldo Emerson: "Failure is but a steppingstone to success." [13]

At age 15 I heard Oral Roberts preach a sermon entitled "You Can't Go Under for Going Over" from the text where Jesus said, "Let us go across to the other side." In the biblical setting, Jesus rebuked His disciples for being fearful in a storm on the Sea of Galilee while He slept: "Why are you afraid? Have you no faith?" (Mark 4:35-40). I never forgot that sermon. Any time you can make someone stand up on the inside, you have increased your chances of winning him to your church; and more important, you have a better chance of leading him to Christ.

The second type of esteem need relates to others. Each of us wears an invisible sign on his lapel that says, "I want to be complimented." Most of us disdain pretentious flattery, particularly if we perceive a hidden motive. We are unimpressed if a person is lathering us before a shave, or buttering us up only to get us to do something. We all, however, appreciate sincere compliments. "Look at me," we are all unconsciously crying, "and see that of the more than 4 billion persons

---

[12] Jess Lair, *I Ain't Much, Baby—But I'm All I've Got* (Greenwich, Conn.: Faucett Publications, Inc., 1972).

[13] Essay on "Self-Reliance."

on this planet, I am unique. Like each snowflake, I am different. Take time to observe that difference."[14]

Of course, the need extends far beyond compliments and involves a desire for reputation, prestige, status, fame, glory, dominance, recognition, attention, importance, dignity, and appreciation.

The experienced fund-raiser knows that you sell recognition, glory, and fame as much as the project. I am thinking of a certain private religious university whose buildings are valued at $100 million. Buildings are named after major benefactors. Wings of buildings are named after substantial contributors. Rooms are named after donors with a picture of the donor framed on the wall. Of course, there is a sentence that says, "To God be all the glory," before listing every contributor on a huge gold-plated plaque. Yet obviously, we want some of the glory, too!

Two distinct Jewish castes or social classes were familiar to people in first-century Palestine: (1) the *haberim* and (2) the *amme ha-arez*. The *haberim* were generally educated and economically comfortable Jews, who were superciliously punctilious in the observance of tithing, conduct, Kosher rules, and ritual cleanliness. This group included the scribes and Pharisees who followed the oral law of the Mishnah rather than the written law of the Torah (the Pentateuch or first five books of the Old Testament). The Mishnah was an interpretation and augmentation of the Torah adapted to daily life and put into writing after the fall of Jerusalem in A.D. 70. The Mishnah and the Gemara

---

[14] The world population reached 4 billion in 1975 and was increasing at the annual rate of 2 percent.

comprise the Talmud (sixty-three books of laws and ethical lore). Jesus accused this group of ostentatious display of piety while substituting the tradition of teachers for the Word of God (Matthew 6:1-16; Mark 7:6-8; *et al*).

The second caste, the *amme ha-arez* (literally, "people of the land") were by far the most populous. This group was generally uneducated and often illiterate. With few exceptions, like tax collectors, they were the poor, the masses of laborers, the nonpracticing Jews, and the ones most attracted to the ministry of Christ. The *haberim* did not associate socially with the *amme ha-arez*, and intermarriage was almost as unthinkable as with a Gentile. The contempt of the upper caste for the lower caste can be felt in the Gospel of John: "Have any of the authorities or of the Pharisees [members of the *haberim*] believed in him [Jesus]? But this crowd [*amme ha-arez*], who do not know the law [the oral tradition of the Mishnah], are accursed" (John 7:48). Contemporary Jewish literature denied these "accursed" any type of resurrection.[15] They were thought to be unworthy of divine care.

When Jesus championed the cause of the crowd as He frequently did, He was obviously appealing to their esteem needs. When Jesus said, "The sabbath was made for man, not man for the sabbath" (Mark 2:27), He was attacking the *haberim* who would walk 3,333 feet on the seventh day and no more, who would not set a broken bone, light a fire, gargle, or look in a mirror on Saturday. The two most famous rabbis in the generation immediately preceding Jesus, Hillel and

---

[15] Kethuboth IIIb.

Shammai, even squabbled about whether an egg laid by a hen on the Sabbath could be eaten.[16] When the people of the land heard Jesus poke fun at the absurdities of the Mishnah, they felt a little more important.

When Jesus ridiculed long prayers on street corners and mocked the observance of ceremonial rituals, members of the crowd stood a little taller (Matthew 6:15, 16). When Jesus called the *haberim*, "white-walled sepulchres," claiming that their piety was insufficient to obtain eternal life, and proclaimed that the kingdom of God belonged to the poor, the crowd undoubtedly felt a surge of pride (Luke 6:20). Ego needs long suppressed were certainly released.

Little wonder that the followers of Jesus came almost exclusively from the lower caste! It was the commoners who quickened to attention when Jesus remarked that not even a sparrow falls without the Father's notice and how much more important were they than sparrows (Matthew 10:29-31)! It was the normally bustling crowd that sat in silence straining to hear every word when Jesus told them that they were so important that God counted each hair on their head (Matthew 10:30). The Jewish scholar, Kaufmann Kohler, attributes the success of the early Christian church to its esteem appeal aimed at the masses, contrasted with the contemptuous and hostile attitude of the Pharisees.[17]

---

[16] A. T. Robertson's *The Pharisees and Jesus* is a classic on the subject. See also *The Jewish World in the Time of Jesus* (New York, 1939) by C. A. H. Guignebert, p. 796, and *The Jewish People in the Time of Jesus Christ*, by Schuerer, esp. Div. II, Vol. II, pp. 96-105.

[17] *The Jewish Encyclopedia*, I, 484.

There is nothing worldly or inappropriate in appealing to esteem needs. Appreciation, for example, is the lubricant in the machinery of life. So much did Jesus appreciate the anonymous woman who poured upon His head the "alabaster jar of very expensive ointment" that He promised a memorial to her deed wherever the gospel is preached (Matthew 26:6-13). Paul and Luke appreciated the honor received on the island of Malta (Acts 28:10).

The Bible tells us to honor or esteem (Greek *time)* our parents (Matthew 15:4), to "outdo one another in showing honor (Romans 12:10), to esteem all men as human beings and especially those in authority such as emperors (1 Peter 2:17). Wives who were considered chattel, just another article of property, were now to be esteemed by their husbands (1 Peter 3:7). Ministers engaged in preaching or teaching are worthy of "double honor" (1 Timothy 5:17). Those who "seek . . . honor" by "well-doing" are promised eternal life (Romans 2:7). If we follow the admonitions of Jesus to expose our light to the world that men might see our good works, we are sure to get some appreciation in the process (Matthew 5:16). Every church should have Pastor Appreciation Sunday. Every Sunday school should give its teachers an appreciation present. With a little ingenuity, we can think of hundreds of ways to obey the Scripture to give "honor to whom honor is due" (Romans 13:7).

The Bible assures us that God will not forget our work and labor of love (Hebrews 6:10). God has us not only on His hands and in His heart, but also on His mind. And what a gospel we have to relate to the esteem needs of man! God values the soul of each person more than the aggregate wealth of the world

(Matthew 16:26). Each person has an opportunity to become royalty, a child of God, an heir of God, and a joint heir with Jesus Christ (Romans 8:17). Christians are "a chosen race, a royal priesthood, a holy nation," says the Bible. "Once you were no people but now you are God's people" (1 Peter 2:9, 10). The New Testament message of adoption, new birth, and sonship provides an inexhaustible source for appeal to esteem needs. Everybody, even though nobody, becomes somebody when he or she accepts Christ.

APPEALING TO SELF-ACTUALIZATION NEEDS

If our other needs are substantially met, the need for self-actualization becomes most important. This term, first used by Kurt Goldstein, and popularized by Abraham Maslow in psychology and Douglas McGregor in industry, pertains to self-fulfillment or self-realization.

For many this need is latent and dormant. Jesus described the role of a typical servant in first-century Palestine. First, he worked all day in the field plowing. Of course, this was strenuous labor, holding a simple wooden plow behind an ox or ass. At evening the servant returned home only to face the task of preparing supper for the master and serving his table before he himself could eat. And all this without thanks, Jesus said, because it was expected as part of his job description (Luke 17:7-9). For such a person, there was little energy expended deciding whether to leave the hovel provided or to seek prestigious accommodations. Nor was there much time spent existentially contemplating the philosophical issues of life. He was born a servant and would die a servant, and his children would be servants. Basic needs pressing upon him, higher-level needs were asleep.

In underdeveloped countries where workers often live under subsistence conditions, higher-level needs are as dormant as those of the Palestinian servant. A study of 200 factory workers in India showed a concern only for job security, earnings, and personal benefits—all lower-order needs.[18] A study of blue-collar workers in two industries here in the United States showed major concerns to be at lower levels.[19] Another study, a comparison between blue-collar and white-collar workers at comparable salary levels, showed security, love, or belonging needs of primary concern for the first, while self-actualization concerns were foremost for the second.[20] Apparently, the cultural influences of blue-collar occupations, along with union emphases, shape the dominant needs more than the amount of paycheck or level of accomplishment.

In studies with managers in both the United States and England, top-level needs completely dominate the employment struggle. From lower-level needs to upper-

---

[18] Paras Nath Singh and Robert J. Wherry, Sr., "Ranking of Job Factors by Factory Workers in India," *Personnel Psychology* (Spring, 1963), 29-33.

[19] M. Schwart, E. Jenusaitis, and H. Startk, "A Comparison of the Perception of Job-related Needs in Two Industry Groups," *Personnel Psychology* (Summer, 1966), 188. The study involved 154 utility and 113 manufacturing workers. First-level supervisors also ranked similarly.

[20] Frank Friedlander, "Comparative Work Value Systems," *Personnel Psychology* (Spring, 1965), 1-20. Research included almost 1,500 government workers. See also Michael Beer, "Needs and Need Satisfaction Among Clerical Workers in Complex and Routine Jobs," *Personnel Psychology* (Summer, 1968), 209-222.

level needs, security, love, esteem and self-actualization needs are each in turn progressively less satisfied.[21] As might be expected, bottom-level managers or first-level supervisors are less satisfied than middle-level managers because of fewer privileges of rank and lesser opportunity to satisfy awakened higher-level needs.[22] A study showed that persons in the professions of medicine, university teaching, and law were concerned most with self-actualization.[23] A study by the author showed the same to be true for ministers, priests, and rabbis.[24]

Self-actualization, self-fulfillment, or self-realization needs are divided into two main types: The first relates to adventure, excitement, change, curiosity, and pleasure. The second pertains to such concepts as meaningfulness, purpose, direction, value system, constructiveness, creativeness, ambition, independence, growth, enrichment, and development.

The first aspect of this need is often ephemeral, transitory, fleeting, and momentary—the kind of thing that can be satisfied by participating in a tennis match,

---

[21] Mason Haire, Edwin E. Ghiselli, Lyman W. Porter, "Cultural Patterns in the Role of the Manager," *Industrial Relations* (February, 1963), 113. The survey covers 2,800 managers in 11 countries including the United States, England, Continental Europe, and Japan.

[22] Lyman W. Porter, "A Study of Perceived Need Satisfactions in Bottom and Middle Management Jobs," *Journal of Applied Psychology* (February, 1961), 1-10. See also Larry L. Cummings and Aly M. Eisalmi, "The Impact of Role Diversity, Job Level, and Organizational Size in Managerial Satisfaction," *Administrative Science Quarterly* (March, 1970), 1-10. See also J. B. Rhinehart; *et al*, "Comparative Study of Need Satisfactions in Government and Business Hierarchies," *Journal of Applied Psychology* (June, 1969), 230-235.

[23] Boris Blai, Jr., "A Job Satisfaction Predictor," *Personnel Journal* (October, 1963), 453-456.

[24] Richard L. Stoppe, "What Motivates the Clergy?" Unpublished Study (May, 1975). The sample included 100 clergymen of varying denominations.

gliding down a turbulent river in a canoe, mountain climbing, a vacation to the Mexican Riviera, rearranging the household furniture, reading an exciting novel, buying a new sports car, or the like.

Much of this adventure and excitement can be experienced vicariously. Seventy-three million persons watched the Superbowl this year via television—more than watched the first landing on the moon! (Since this type of need is generally met outside the job, studies showing a difference between blue-collar and white-collar workers, and a difference between supervisor and subordinate, are not applicable here.) Two of the greatest success stories in advertising history were the change from beverage appeals associated with the physical, such as thirst and taste, to appeals associated with adventure; for example, "You only go around once in life, so you have to reach out for all the gusto you can get."[25]

Much of religious emphasis has been directed toward self-denial, self-crucifixion, negativism, and abstinence. And there is this emphasis of Scripture. Jesus said to disciples matured by three years of teaching: "If any man would come after me, let him deny himself and take up his cross and follow me" (Matthew 16:24). Paul wrote to the members of the Church at Rome: "We know that our old self was crucified" (Romans 6:6). And to the churches of Galatia Paul testified, "I have been crucified with Christ" (Galatians 2:20). I have heard Billy Graham attempt to communicate this concept in modern terms by saying, "We must take up our electric chair."

---

[25] Schlitz commercial. The greatest success story was the advertisement of Colt 45 malt liquor.

I do not deny this emphasis of Scripture. I do deny, however, that this emphasis means that Christians should adopt the nit-picking, gnat-straining, mote-removing messages and practices of the Pharisees. Christ's most scathing words were reserved for condemnation of legalism and all its trifling tests of sanctification and pious devotion! Preachers of such a gospel, Jesus called, "child[ren] of hell," "[a] brood of vipers," and "whitewashed tombs" (Matthew 23:15, 27, 33).

I also deny that Paul advocated religious legalism. Paul asked the Church at Colosse, "Why do you submit to regulations, 'Do not handle, Do not taste, Do not touch' . . . ? These have indeed an *appearance* of wisdom in promoting rigor of devotion and self-abasement and severity of the body, but *they are of no value* in checking the indulgence of the flesh" (Colossians 2:20-23). To the Church of Corinth, Paul rejected the idea that true religion is a court sentence of petty proscriptions (1 Corinthians 6:12).

The Christian way is the adventure of a lifetime and more! Jesus explained that He came so we might "have life, and have it abundantly" (John 10:10). Not everything that is fun is sinful. Not everything human is worldly or of the devil. Christ has brought life with a capital *L*. He promised that if we would lose our life for His sake, we would really find it (Matthew 16:25). One fruit of the spiritual life is joy (Galatians 5:22; Romans 14:17). Nehemiah preached that "the joy of the Lord is your strength" (Nehemiah 8:10). The Psalmist sang of the "fulness of joy" found in God's presence and the "pleasures for evermore" experienced at His right hand (Psalm 16:11).

If the church is dullsville, it is a reflection on us, not on the gospel message or the spiritual life. We have done so little with so much. Too often we move along in the same predictable pattern, Sunday after Sunday, year after year. We must vary our programs, try different things, promote exciting things. We must be creative. Ornithologists tell us that even a bird is unhappy if it has only one song. We must reach out for all the vibrance that we, or our congregation, or Sunday school class, or youth group can get. It is there at the Father's right hand!

The second aspect of self-actualization is the more permanent and long-range concept of self-fulfillment or self-realization. It involves maturation, growth, the integration of personality, zestful and harmonious living. It also involves a reaching for the potentiality of one's talents and abilities and the freedom to find that potentiality. What a man *can* be he *must* be. It further involves the philosophical questions: Why am I here? What is the ultimate purpose of my life? Is the achievement or goal I am seeking worthwhile? What is the real meaning of life? What are the permanent values? What are the truths that time and circumstances cannot alter?

Self-actualized persons experience life vividly with complete concentration and total absorption. They are existential in their Christian experience; that is, they enjoy the present moments of their salvation fully instead of only making preparation for the next life or the coming of the Lord.

Self-actualized persons are aware of their real selves. They shun masks and self-deception. They identify their unhealthy defense mechanisms and abandon them.

Self-actualized persons take responsibility for themselves and their choices. They feel no pressure to conform to worldly norms, for they have a well-developed set of spiritual norms. They are not uncomfortable with others who do not follow their standards. They simply let their light shine while identifying with the conditions of others.

Self-actualized persons make growth choices. They seek to maximize wholeness of personality. They seek competence physically, emotionally, intellectually, and spiritually. They seek to integrate their ideal self with their real self.

Self-actualized persons are victorious in their Christian living. Theirs is the abundant life, and they leave their healing touch wherever they go.

Much of the teaching of Jesus was designed to raise His listeners to a more triumphant level of living. He taught a gospel of the abundant and victorious life from which Paul undoubtedly derived the concept of being "more than conquerors" (Romans 8:37).

Persons in Christ's day chafed under the imperial Roman rule that a man at any time could be compelled to carry mail for one mile. Jesus told them, "If any one forces you to go one mile, go with him two miles" (Matthew 5:41). Take the sting, bitterness, and resentment out of the first mile of command, Jesus was saying, by going beyond the call of duty and exercising your freedom in the second mile.

"How often shall my brother sin against me, and I forgive him?" Peter asked Jesus. Surely seven times would be the uppermost limit, Peter reasoned. Jesus replied, "Seventy times seven," an Aramaic expression meaning "innumerably" (Matthew 18:21-22). Jesus was teaching that the unforgiving spirit hurts most the one who harbors it, that turning the other cheek to wrong softens the first punch (Matthew 5:39). Overcoming evil with good (Romans 12:21) is not merely the best way; it is the only successful way of effecting moral change!

Christians must learn to witness, teach, and preach this aspect of Christ's message. There is a tremendous appeal to growth and maturation here.

There is a penalty in hate and resentment. It is not what you eat that generally makes you sick; it is what eats you. Filet mignon, potatoes au gratin, and asparagus au hollandaise followed by strawberry cheese cake a la mode might just as well be stale bread and water if eaten with malice. Solomon noted that a dish of herbs was a better meal with love than the best beef eaten with hatred (Proverbs 15:17).

On one occasion the Pharisees demanded to know from Jesus when the kingdom of God should come. Jesus explained that the Kingdom was not something that came with observation. Rather "the kingdom of God is *within* [Greek *entos*] you" (Luke 17:20, 21). Jesus was saying that the laws of our being are the laws of God. These laws are not imposed upon us extrinsically but are inherent in our physiological and psychological constitution. No wonder 75 to 85 percent of sickness has a psychological rather than an organic base.

When an engineer designs an engine, it only works effectively as he designed it to work. When God made man, He placed His stamp of design upon him. The Old Testament calls it being made in the image of God. If we discover the laws of God's design and live accordingly, we live abundantly. To live otherwise is to court disaster.

A locomotive is designed to travel on rails. On the rails it finds its potential to function, to pull its load, and to reach its destination. If the locomotive should jump the tracks in search of freedom, if it should desire to explore a meadow and brook, it loses all power and faces ruin.

God has stamped His image upon us. His laws are written within us. Hence the Bible can say, "The teaching of the wise is a fountain of life" (Proverbs 13:14). It can also say that "the way of transgressors is hard" (Proverbs 13:15, KJV). To go against the Kingdom within us is to jaywalk, to go against the lights, inviting tragedy. Evil is not harmonious with the universe. The Bible poetically speaks of the stars in their courses fighting against the evil Sisera (Judges 5:20).

Some translations read, "The kingdom of God is *among* you." Which is correct? The Greek will support either translation. Both concepts are equally valid. God has placed His stamp upon our social relationship as well as our physiological and psychological constitution. The Bible also says, "A man who is kind benefits himself, but a cruel man hurts himself" (Proverbs 11:17). The only way we can get along with ourselves and with other people is God's way. So many principles taught in psychology and interpersonal communication courses are but extensions of principles taught in God's Word.

James and John were petty individuals, selfish, wanting a special place in Christ's kingdom. They were revengeful, wanting to call down fire from heaven as Elijah did, to consume the misguided people of Samaria. But how they were transformed! John wrote more about love than any other New Testament writer.

Both James and John learned that the kingdom of God was a ruling power "among them." They learned that the spirit of Elijah was not the spirit of Christ (Luke 9:54, 55).

Wayne State University is a metropolitan school in Detroit with an enrollment of around 30,000 students. A recent study showed that the average age of its undergraduate student was 26. One part-time student was 87 years old. The oldest full-time student was an ambitious 82. Older people are going to college. Women, who for years fulfilled home responsibilities, are going back to college for further personal development and fulfillment now that the children are attending school. Others are enriching their lives through meaningful volunteer programs. Here again, the church or some related program can become a means of fulfillment and deep satisfaction.

Regarding the ultimate questions of life, the world has given pathetic answers.

A humanist writes:

The dim and shadowy outline of a superhuman deity fades slowly away from before us; and as the mist of his presence floats aside, we perceive with greater and greater clearness the shape of a yet grander and nobler figure—of him who made all gods and shall unmake them. From the dim dawn of history and from the inmost depth of every soul, the face of our father Man looks out upon us with the fire of eternal youth in his eyes, and says, "Before Jehovah was, I am."[26]

---

[26] W. K. Clifford, "The Ethics of Religion," *Lectures and Essays*, ed. L. Stephens and F. Pollock, (London: Macmillan Co., 1879), II, p. 348.

John Dewey, one of the fathers of modern educational theory, has suggested that we offer the world "a religion without a God."[27]

Eric Fromm, a neo-Freudian psychologist writes:

There is only one solution to man's problem: to face the truth, to acknowledge his fundamental aloneness and solitude in a universe indifferent to his fate, to recognize that there is no meaning to life except the meaning man gives his life by the unfolding of his powers by living productively.[28]

The philosopher Bertrand Russell writes:

The world in which we live can be understood as a result of muddle and accident; but if it is the outcome of deliberate purpose, the purpose must have been that of a fiend. For my part, I find accident a less painful and more plausible hypothesis.[29]

The famous French novelist Albert Camus suggests that life is one continuous worthless struggle. Life is pushing a heavy ball up a steep hill, Camus says, only to have it roll back on you. And the whole process begins over and over again.[30]

The famous playwright Jean Paul Sartre pictures life as an insoluble human dilemma from which there is

---

[27] John Dewey, *A Common Faith* (New Haven: Yale University Press, 1934), p. 50.

[28] Eric Fromm, *Man for Himself* (New York: Holt, Rinehart, & Winston, 1947), pp. 44, 45.

[29] Bertrand Russell, *Why I Am Not a Christian* (New York: Simon and Schuster, 1957).

[30] Albert Camus, *Le Mythe de Sisyphe* (The Myth of Sisyphe), 1942.

"no exit" other than death.[31] Eugene Ionesco devotes his entire play *The Chairs* to telling the supposed true meaning of life. In the final moments "the orator" faces the audience and says it all, "Blaaaah!" and the curtain closes. The Black playwright LeRoi Jones writes that life is like an unkept public "toilet," full of foul odors and nothing more.[32]

How much better the Christian answer! Lloyd C. Douglas, author of *The Robe* and *The Big Fisherman*, writes:

Confidently we make our way by the light of that Galilean Torch even into the deepening shadows of life's inevitable evening calmly and unafraid. I do not pretend to understand the full mystery of his light; but I do know that by its radiance I can see. And I hold with the full intellectual pride of one critical of facts until they have been adequately verified, to a belief that allows me to trust that ineffable radiance all the way and into a world beyond. So if I stoop into a dark tremendous sea of cloud, it is but for a time; I press God's lamp close to my breast—its splendour, soon or late, will pierce the gloom: I shall emerge one day![33]

The Christian message, more than any other, answers the ultimate questions of life. The Bible promises, "In all thy ways acknowledge him, and he shall direct thy paths" (Proverbs 3:6, KJV).

---

[31] Jean Paul Sartre, *No Exit* (1946).

[32] LeRoi Jones (now Imamu Baraka), *The Toilet* (1965).

[33] Lloyd C. Douglas, *Those Disturbing Miracles* (New York: Harper & Bros., 1927), pp. 259-60.

CONCLUSION

It is characteristic of man that throughout life he is desiring something. Satisfy one need and another quickly emerges. Man yearns consciously for that which might realistically be attained. The factor of attainment is crucial for understanding the differences in motivations between various classes within our own population and between the United States and other poorer countries and cultures.

Needs are dynamic rather than static, so that one might be motivated at various levels simultaneously or in rapid succession. Sometimes a conflict of needs arises causing motivation in two opposite directions at once, such as occurred with the rich young ruler who considered following Christ (Luke 18:18).

George Washington once said, "The people must feel before they can see." Modern communicational psychologists agree with the first President. Persuasion is the process of securing acceptance of an idea or getting someone to act in some specific way by identifying that idea or action with one's needs, motives, and desires. An appeal to a reason is effective only to the extent that it is also an appeal to a want.

When we preach the gospel and witness to its truth, we are totally dependent upon the Holy Spirit. No amount of human skill can ever transform the human heart. But we can, through a knowledge of man's needs, be led by the Holy Spirit to present the gospel in its most attractive cover to the people we meet. Here Jesus' words are so applicable: "The sons of this world are wiser in their own generation than the sons of light" (Luke 16:8). Let us follow the example of Christ. Let us present the gospel as it is—irresistibly attractive. Remember, the gospel is like an ocean meeting the shoreline of human need at every point.

Figure 1-1 gives a graphic review of the five most dominant needs of man in order of their strength if not satisfied. Figure 1-2 gives a graphic review of those needs for the majority of persons living in the United States. The order is reversed because our lower needs are predominantly satisfied. A satisfied need is no longer a motivator. As the figure shows, appeals to self-actualization, esteem, and affiliative needs are most persuasive.

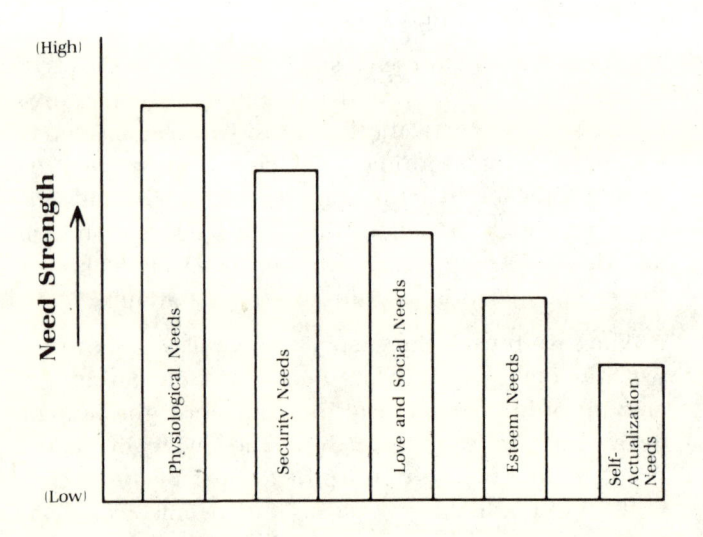

FIGURE 1-1. MASLOW'S NEED HIERARCHY

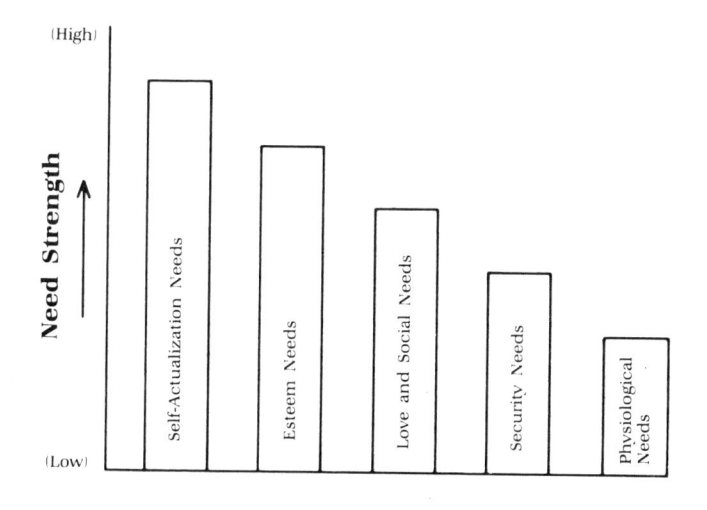

FIGURE 1-2. THE STRENGTH OF NEEDS IN THE U.S.

2

THE ELEMENT OF TRUST

Trust is indispensable to an effective communicative climate. To trust and to earn another's trust is like turning on the public address system, or turning up the volume of the radio. Trust allows the other to hear!

A mother who had reared an exceptional family of 11 children, all achievers, was asked her formula of success. "I just trusted them," she answered.

Trust builds the mutual respect and confidence necessary for open, honest communication, vital to any interpersonal relationship—between parent and child, husband and wife, between lovers, between friends, between supervisor and subordinate, and also between a minister and his congregation.

COMMUNICATIVE CLIMATE

The Bible records an astonishing failure in the ministry of Jesus! He was unsuccessful in Nazareth, a Prophet without honor in His own home town. His ministry, which thrilled the hearts of multitudes elsewhere, fell on deaf ears in Nazareth. Even worse, the townspeople were offended that a carpenter's Son would dare preach to them. He should be at the shop making yokes and plows! In Nazareth Jesus experienced a hostile environment, an unproductive climate that tied His hands. He could do few mighty works there because of their unbelief (Matthew 13:58).

Climate is more important to success than words. Although you communicate in the tongues of men and of angels, if you have a poor psychological environment, you will sound like a noisy gong or a clanging cymbal (read 1 Corinthians 13:1). Climate is more important than technique. The best organizational arrangement, the most dynamic delivery, and the most inspiring vocabulary profit little in a poor communicative climate. On the other hand, even poor communication has a fair chance of success in a good climate.

Climate cannot be ignored. Every latitude has its climate. So does every home, every organization, every church. Some kind of climate graces or disgraces every meeting, every group, every conversation, every meal, every sermon, every song.

Climate differs from weather in terms of duration. Here climate refers to the psychological environment over a long period of time. Hence, we are not talking about one day's high or low. We are not talking about one day's stormy outburst or peak relationship. We are talking about climate generated by leadership and interpersonal communication over months and years!

Meteorologically, climate describes data such as temperature, precipitation, humidity, wind, barometric pressure, cloudiness, and visibility. Climate determines all flora and fauna from the simplest one-celled forms of life, algae and protozoa, to the laboratory-developed orange groves of Florida and wheat fields of Kansas to the insects, reptiles, birds, and mammals. For example, the malaria carrier Anopheles mosquito cannot breed at temperatures below 61 degrees Fahrenheit or at a relative humidity under 63 percent; the northern limit for oranges is the July isotherm of 72 degrees Fahrenheit; and wheat will not grow where the annual rainfall exceeds 40 inches.

Communicative climate is as important to emotional life as the weather is to physical life. Communicatively, climate describes qualities such as trust, love, provisionalism, acceptance, active listening, empathic understanding, positive attitudes, recognition, and respect. A barometer of human needs, communicative climate concerns itself with potential that clamors for fulfillment—with motivation to become, to grow, to achieve. Communicative climate refers to interpersonal relationships where people both heal and hurt, restore and deplete, help and hinder, where people grow and flourish or shrivel and die. For example, if management or leadership displays the cluster of traits described in our definition, it correlates significantly with productivity, creativity, cooperation, and job satisfaction in labor.

People are always reacting to others—positively, negatively, or indifferently. Some by their very presence make others feel important, alive, and capable of unimagined spiritual and personal growth.

How important is communicative climate? Consider the home. Research studies show that pervasive parental attitudes and *"the overall atmosphere of the home, rather than specific training practices most"* determine optimum child development.[1]

The following poem by Dorothy Law Nolte would make an excellent introduction to a course in child psychology.

CHILDREN LEARN WHAT THEY LIVE

*If a child lives with criticism,
    he learns to condemn.
If a child lives with hostility,
    he learns to fight.
If a child lives with fear,
    he learns to be apprehensive.
If a child lives with pity,
    he learns to feel sorry for himself.
If a child lives with ridicule,
    he learns to be shy.
If a child lives with jealousy,
    he learns what envy is.
If a child lives with shame,
    he learns to feel guilty.
If a child lives with encouragement,
    he learns to be confident.*

---

[1] Harold W. Bernard, *Mental Health in the Classroom* (New York: McGraw-Hill, 1970), p. 216. (Italics mine.)

*If a child lives with tolerance,
he learns to be patient.
If a child lives with praise,
he learns to be appreciative.
If a child lives with acceptance,
he learns to love.
If a child lives with approval,
he learns to like himself.
If a child lives with recognition,
he learns that it is good to have a goal.
If a child lives with sharing,
he learns about generosity.
If a child lives with honesty and fairness,
he learns what truth and justice are.
If a child lives with security,
he learns to have faith in himself and
in those about him.
If a child lives with friendliness,
he learns that the world is a nice place
in which to live.
If you live with serenity,
your child will live with peace of mind.*

With what is your child living?

If we turn from the home to the school, studies of the characteristics of effective teachers point to a similar conclusion: *The human climate for learning is more important than the specific teaching procedures adopted.*[2] Numerous experimental studies confirm that

---

[2] David G. Ryans, *Characteristics of Teachers: A Research Study* (Washington, D.C.: American Council on Education, 1960), pp. 365-366.

pupils learn what a teacher is as well as what he says. Pupils unconsciously absorb attitudes, reflect moods, and come to share convictions and imitate behavior of teachers.[3] Problems such as motivation, discipline, social interaction, pupil achievement, and above all the continuing desire to learn center in the learning climate.[4]

In business and industry the same story emerges. The climate often spells success or failure.[5] Some years ago, one of our industrial giants established experimental plants to test the results of supportive management and communicative climate. Already-efficient plants were designated control units. After seven years of testing, the results were incredible. The average cost per item in the control plants was 70 cents; but in the experimental plants, only 22 cents. The control plants needed 17 to 23 managers; the experimental, three to five for comparable units.[6]

How important, then, is communicative climate? For the Christian home, school, church, or organization, it is paramount. Therefore, consider with me some of the many ingredients of communicative climate.

---

[3] Harold W. Bernard, *Psychology of Learning and Teaching*, 1972 ed., Chapter 1.

[4] Carl Rogers, *Freedom to Learn* (Columbus, Ohio: Charles E. Merrill Publishing Co., 1968).

[5] This concept is supported by the numerous management studies summarized by William B. Haney, *Communication and Organizational Behavior*, 3rd ed. (Homewood, Ill.: Irwin, Inc., 1974).

[6] Carl Rogers, *On Personal Power* (New York: Delacorte Press, 1977), pp. 100-102.

ORGANIZATIONAL EFFECTIVENESS

In a study of 14 organizations of various kinds and sizes, mutual trust between supervisors and subordinates emerged as the key variable to both communication and performance.[7] A larger study of 5,000 organizations substantiates the same conclusion: technical and managerial competence being equal, trust is the key variable of organizational effectiveness.[8]

A supervisor's trust in a subordinate begins a chain of positive reinforcement: trust ⟶ improved communication ⟶ higher productivity ⟶ greater trust ⟶ even better communication ⟶ still higher productivity. Conversely, distrust reinforces a negative cycle featuring poor communication, rigid supervision, and low productivity. "I knew I couldn't trust that bum anyway," says the boss. What follows is a worsening climate for communication and even lower productivity due in part to job dissatisfaction, a high rate of absenteeism, and costly turnovers.

In manager-subordinate, leader-member relationships, studies show that trust is formed by one's perception in four broad categories: (1) reliability, (2) dynamism, (3) expertise, and (4) character.

1. Reliability. Reliability concerns dependability in two areas: (a) job expectations and (b) interpersonal expectations.

Our job expectations are dependent, to a large degree, upon our position and qualifications. In general we expect fairness: equal pay for equal work,

---

[7] Haney, *op. cit.*, p. 12.
[8] Rensis Likert, *New Patterns of Management* (New York: McGraw-Hill, 1961), p. 101.

reward for diligence, opportunity for promotion and advancement, and recognition for achievement. We expect our jobs to be enriched when we gain experience and promotion. Enrichment includes increased responsibility for new and more difficult tasks, accountability for one's own work, authority to make important decisions, freedom from rigid control, and the assignment of specialized tasks in which we can become an expert, allowing for growth and development. The fulfillment of these expectations increases the trust of subordinates and members in managers and leaders.

Managers also have a job expectations of subordinates. These include a full day's work for a full day's pay, dependability within the job description, punctuality, the meeting of deadlines, quality work, and an identification with organizational goals and objectives. The fulfillment of these expectations increases the trust of managers and leaders in subordinates and members.

Interpersonal expectations are important also. We trust our superiors and leaders to the extent that they treat us with dignity and respect. We tend to equate trustworthiness with kindness, unselfishness, praise, patience, openness, and responsiveness to our emotional needs.

Managers and leaders also have interpersonal expectations that determine trust in subordinates and followers. We, too, expect kindness, unselfishness, openness, patience, and praise. The minister expects, for example (and rightly so), that members express appreciation for a sermon that meets their spiritual needs. Managers and leaders especially look for loyalty and respect. We expect, for example, that complaints will be brought to our attention rather than taken to our superior. We expect that we will not be criticized negatively behind our backs. And we want respect. So often the leader mistakenly throws the weight of his position and authority around just trying to get respect!

Reliability regarding interpersonal expectations is vital to trust between friends and between lovers. A woman might rightly expect her husband and friends to compliment her new hair style. Spouses expect the loyalty of faithfulness. And we all want to be treated with dignity and respect. We choose our friends on the basis of how much they can be trusted or relied on to meet our interpersonal needs. We also choose our church, organization, or job to the extent it can be trusted to meet our reliability expectations. We often change friends, churches, and jobs when these expectations are frustrated.

2. *Dynamism.* Managers and leaders are trusted in proportion to their subordinates' perception of them as dynamic. This is true because of our cultural expectations regarding leadership. A cluster of characteristics determines our perception of dynamism. We trust the leader who is emphatic, rather than hesitant; active, rather than passive; quick to understand and think on his feet, rather than slow; assertive (not aggressive), rather than acquiescent; bold, rather than timid; extroverted, rather than withdrawn in speech or manner; energetic, rather than lethargic; frank, rather than evasive; and open-minded, rather than dogmatic. We trust the leader who is forceful and vigorous and who takes initiative. We look for positive attitudes and enthusiasm about life in general and about organizational

goals and objectives in particular. In short, we look for charisma, a quality of leadership that captures the imagination and inspires allegiance and devotion.

3. *Expertise.* Expertise is competence or ability. It is judged by our perception of one's intelligence, education, formal degrees, training, experience, and general knowledge. Since we often cannot judge a person's competence in his own field because of our lack of knowledge, we subconsciously make judgments on the basis of our own area of competence. Few church members, for example, would question the minister's knowledge by his exegesis or interpretation of Scripture. The average layman is not capable of making an intelligent challenge here—and he knows it! The minister's expertise is judged (often erroneously) by his excursions into such things as current affairs or illustrations familiar to his audience. He will be judged by his fluency and delivery. When a person perceives that we are up-to-date, well informed, fluent, accurate in our general knowledge, or knowledgeable in an area of his competence, our trust level or credibility rises.

Expertise is also judged by one's past record and positions held, and by one's present achievement, success, and accomplishment. At lower levels in an organization, expertise is viewed more in terms of technical skills. A foreman, for example, must know how to do anything his workers can. He was promoted to foreman because of his skills as a worker. As one advances in an organization, his expertise is winnowed by conceptual skills such as planning, organizing, coordinating, forecasting, motivating, informing, persuading, clarifying, arbitrating, and promoting need satisfaction. Trust does not come automatically with authority or position. It must be earned every day.

4. *Character.* "What you are speaks so loudly I cannot hear what you are saying." This aphorism is especially true regarding Christian communication and organizational leadership. We trust the person of integrity. We expect behavior to match communication. We look for sincerity and honesty, expecting a person's word to be his bond. Character becomes increasingly important, either negatively or positively, the longer we serve an organization and the better people know us.

It was the 1963 Whitemarsh Open Golf Tournament in Philadelphia. Arnold Palmer astonished the galleries and officials by claiming a one-stroke penalty for himself on the first hole. When questioned, he explained, "I saw the ball move slightly when I addressed it." Palmer jettisoned thousands of dollars in prize money for an infraction no one else saw. Honesty like this made Arnold Palmer a magic name in endorsement advertising.

Honesty inspires trust. Honesty is truthfulness, genuineness, realness, and congruence between word and action. Honesty means openness and the removal of personal facade. It means sincerity like that of Abraham Lincoln. Once he refused a technically good but unjust case. "You'll have to find another lawyer," he said, "because all the time I was standing there talking to the jury, I'd be thinking, 'Lincoln, you're a liar!' And I'm afraid I'd forget myself and say it out loud." Would you have trouble trusting an attorney like that?

MUTUAL TRUST

Mutual trust provides a postive communicative climate in at least four ways:

Trust Lowers Defense Barriers

Criticism tends to be taken constructively and our reporting becomes more accurate because trust lowers the walls of our ego defense mechanisms. A defense mechanism is a device we use to keep from looking at our real feelings or actions. We escape reality by protecting our ego from any disagreeable knowledge of itself. In a threatening climate, we actually delude ourselves to the extent that we no longer are able to be honest with others or with ourselves.

Denial is the child's first line of defense. As both parent and child observe the broken glass of milk, little Suzy, with tears in her eyes and all the sincerity she can summon, denies her participation: "It broke all by itself, Mommy." "I stayed dry all night," says little Johnny, hoping his denial will somehow make the wet bed disappear.

By the time we become adults, our denials have become quite sophisticated. We have learned the art of *rationalization*. Mr. Jones will not say that he was fired because he was doing a poor job, was constantly tardy, and showed open resentment against his boss. That would be too painful to admit. No, the boss was stupid, the job was no good, and he was planning on quitting anyway.

We also use the defense mechanism of *projection*. This is attributing our actions, feeling, or thoughts to someone else. Its most common form is blaming others for our mistakes or inadequacies. Adam tried this excuse with God! "The woman whom [*you* gave] to be with me, *she* gave me fruit of the tree, and I ate" (Genesis 3:12). Eve picked up a tip from Adam and blamed the serpent.

Sometimes our defense is *withdrawal*. We psychologically or physically remove ourselves from threatening or demanding situations. We quit the game and opt for the sidelines. Afraid of failure, we just don't try. Having had an unpleasant experience, we simply refuse to get involved again.

Sometimes our defense mechanism is *regression*. This is reversion to a less-mature behavioral pattern, one we found useful as a child. Name-calling and outbursts of temper fit this category. By shouting, we think we make a weak argument strong.

Of course, there are other defense mechanisms such as *displacing, reaction formation, delusions, compulsions, suppression, hypochondria,* and *psychosomatic symptoms.* In an atmosphere of mutual trust we can examine our unhealthy defense mechanisms and abandon them. We can accept criticism in a positive light and use the energy formerly spent on defense techniques for more profitable steps in self-improvement.

In our reporting, especially to our supervisors, we tend to use three systematic types of distortion to defend our egos: (1) *leveling*—omitting or minimizing some details; (2) *sharpening*—magnifying some details; and (3) *assimilation*—changing information to make the message fit one of our defense mechanisms, our previous attitudes, or the other's expectation. Mutual trust allows us to be more conscious of these tendencies, and to be more accurate in our conversations, reports, and descriptions.

Trust Covers for the Other Person

Trust improves communication because it allows us to cover for each other. Both of us can be spontaneous and express our feelings, while leaving room for mistakes and errors. We hear each other out until our feelings are transparent. We never depart in a huff of unfinished business. Most of all, we trust that neither intends to hurt the other or to be unthoughtful or unkind. If you do something that hurts me, I will cover for you. I will always assume that the offense was inadvertent, was due to personal frustration, perhaps, and never that you wanted to hurt me or "get me." When we trust each other, we can assume good will and proper motive behind all action. With no chips on the shoulder to be knocked off, fewer occasions arise for offense. With no ax to grind, miscommunication due to emotional distortion is mitigated.

Trust Aids Persuasion

Third, trust allows us to be more persuasive. Trust, in terms of reliability, dynamism, expertise, and character, determines credibility. Studies verify that audiences or individuals accept or reject persuasive appeals to a high degree because of the person. The proposition is accepted not necessarily on the basis of logical argument or emotional appeal, but on the basis of trust, respect, and admiration of the speaker.

The identical recorded or written speech given to separate audiences with differing introductions succeeds or fails depending on the source credibility or image of the speaker generated in the introduction. Persuasive power resides in the speaker because of the audience's perception of him. If the speaker is trusted, his speech is logical; if the speaker is not trusted, the same speech is illogical! The higher the trust, the greater the persuasion. When trust is lost, persuasion is lost.

Lyndon Johnson won the 1964 Presidential election by a landslide. He received 486 electoral votes to only 52 for Senator Goldwater, and he carried 44 states and the District of Columbia. Yet four years later, he could not run for reelection. Polls showed he had lost the confidence of the American people because of Vietnam. When Johnson came to office, U.S. forces in Vietnam consisted of 16,300 military advisers. By 1968, American troops in Vietnam numbered over a half million. He had escalated a war he had promised to end. No amount of rhetoric, no public relations campaign could save him.[9]

In the 1972 Presidential campaign, Richard Nixon won reelection by the largest margin in U.S. history—17.75 million votes! Nixon received 520 electoral votes to 17 for McGovern. Yet Nixon could not finish his term of office. He lost the confidence of the American people because of Watergate. Nixon's positive image became such a negative image that he could not support publicly any candidate thereafter without signing that candidate's death warrant!

Trust Allows for Deeper Levels of Communication

Trust provides the climate for the candid expression of ideas and feelings. If feelings are running high, they

---

[9] A good analysis can be found in *The Best and the Brightest* by David Halberstram (New York: Random House, 1972).

must be dealt with before reasoning can take place. Unexpressed feelings cause resentment to build, resulting often in explosions that destroy relationships. If we divide communication into five levels (casual, conversational, emotional, intellectual, and peak), we see that the deeper the trust, the deeper the communication. Let us examine these five levels, proceeding from the lowest to the highest in terms of the amount of trust necessary for each.

a. The Casual Level. This is the level of greetings. It takes little trust to say, "Hi! How are you? What's new?" Most of our communication at any level involves what we may call "strokes" of recognition, attention, respect, warmth, and acceptance.

When my cat brushes up against me, she needs a few strokes of attention. I pet her a few times and she curls up contentedly snuggled against me. If I have been gone all day, however, many more strokes are necessary when I return. She stands on her hind feet stretching her front paws as high as she can reach up my leg. Now she must be picked up and stroked profusely—or she repeats the request!

The casual level of communication involves one or two strokes of recognition, little more. We are offended if these strokes are not given. If an acquaintance has seen us, he had better respond to our "hello" or we are insulted. But if we are asked, "How are you?" he only wants a simple "Fine, thanks." Even a nod will suffice. This is no time to expound at length about your lumbago. If you do, you surely will receive a look that clearly says, "Sorry I asked!"

If while shopping, we meet a casual friend we have not seen for some time, a simple "hi" is insufficient.

More strokes are necessary, so he asks about the children and our recent trip to Hawaii. Don't get carried away, however, and invite him and his wife over for an evening of home movies of the children surfing at Waikiki. That would demonstrate that you misunderstood the intent of a few strokes. Reserve such an invitation for close, understanding friends—friends for whom you are willing to endure the homemade movies of their children diving off the cliffs of Acapulco.

The casual level is shallow and ephemeral, a fulfillment of social amenities. The lion lowers his tail upon greeting any lion stronger than he in the pride, and raises his tail to each one weaker. We say "hi." The military salutes. The lyrics of Paul Simon capture this level of communication:

And in the naked night
I saw ten thousand people, maybe more,
People talking without speaking,
People hearing without listening,
People writing songs that voices never heard.
No one dared disturb the sounds of silence.[10]

b. The Conversational Level. The conversational level involves more strokes than the casual level. In his excellent book *Games People Play*, Dr. Eric Berne describes many of the games we play to stroke each other.[11] People mingle at a party, for example, searching for a group playing or willing to play their game.

---

[10] Paul Simon: music written for *The Graduate*.
[11] Eric Berne, *Games People Play* (New York: Grove Press, 1964).

One popular game is limited to those who have had major operations. Each member listens in rapturous rapport as one by one each describes the ailment, the symptoms, the suffering, the operative procedures, the recovery, and the present restrictions, if any. The social rule is strictly enforced. No one can leave after telling his story until all have had a chance to tell theirs!

In conversation, each gives strokes of attention and recognition, trusting to be stroked in return. Of course, the level of trust is minimal. We can talk at length about current events—a devastating tornado, the new pastor, the Billy Graham crusade—without disclosing much about ourselves.

c. The Emotional Level. A third level of communication is that of emotion. It involves a deeper level of trust because here we risk judgment of our emotional competence.

(1) Emotional Maturity

We have all learned that emotional competence is not the repression of emotion, but rather the constructive expression of emotion. It is the ability to express emotions appropriately and spontaneously while controlling emotional outbursts. Adding to our difficulty is our physiological response to emotion manifesting itself throughout our bodies internally and externally.

When properly channeled, our emotions become our allies and powerful aids to accomplishment. They are like new spark plugs to an automobile engine giving life its flavor, variety, vitality, and motivation. When our emotions are negative, long-lasting, overwhelming, suppressed, pent-up, or improperly channeled, they are like a dirty carburetor disrupting our lives with sputtering and stalling. Emotional maturity is reached when we can react to situations with the appropriate emotion and intensity to serve us, and to let go of those emotions when they have served their purpose.

(2) Anger

Mark records an occasion when Jesus became angry (Mark 3:1-6):

> Again he entered the synagogue, and a man was there who had a withered hand. And they [the Pharisees] watched him, to see whether he would heal him on the sabbath, so that they might accuse him. And he said to the man who had the withered hand, "Come here." And he said to them, "Is it lawful on the sabbath to do good or to do harm, to save life or to kill?" But they were silent. And he looked around at them with anger, grieved at their hardness of heart, and said to the man, "Stretch out your hand." He stretched it out, and his hand was restored. The Pharisees went out, and immediately held counsel with the Herodians against him, how to destroy him.

Notice several things about this incident. First, Jesus chose appropriate emotions for a group hoping to witness a deed on the Sabbath Day so that they might bring formal charges against Him resulting in His death. Jesus chose to be angry and to grieve. Second, Jesus controlled His emotion. He did not punch anyone in the nose. He did not raise His voice. His words were not filled with uncomplimentary adjectives. He confined His anger to a look. Third, He used His anger and grief as an impetus to act positively. He healed the man's withered hand. Fourth, He did not stay angry or distressed. The sun did not set on His wrath (see Ephesians 4:26). Nor did He allow His anger or grief to turn into a negative emotion of hate, resentment, despondency, or depression.

People who spew out a venom of ill feelings toward another person in the name of honesty and openness miss the mark. This does not mean that a person should repress emotion, necessarily, but he should choose an appropriate emotion and channel it toward some constructive purpose. Letting the emotions all hang out, as advocated by some psychologists, neither helps the individual to cope with the problems of life nor clears the air for positive relationships. On the contrary, it hurts; it stings; it separates and divides the body of Christ.

(3) Emotional Control

But what if our emotions overwhelm us? First, we can talk to ourselves. We can say, "That incident just isn't worth getting this upset. I simply choose not to be angry."

Second, we can pray in private where no one can hear us and bare our emotions before the Lord asking Him for release.

Third, we can work or exercise strenuously to relieve the tension in our muscles. I play tennis outside in summer and inside in winter as a means of keeping physically fit and releasing my emotions.

Fourth, if necessary, we can write a vehement letter with forceful expression revealing the intensity of our emotion. But do not—I repeat—do not mail it, ever! Things may look different as early as the next day.

Fifth, as soon as the feeling becomes manageable, we can channel that emotion toward some worthy goal.

(4) Suppression

Suppression may be illustrated by a typical human relations episode familiar to all of us. Suppose that you frequently do something that bothers me. Now, I'm afraid to tell you of my annoyance because I don't wish to hurt you, or I think our relationship will be more peaceful if I keep quiet.

So I keep my feelings inside, and each time you repeat your action I burn and keep score—1 . . . 2 . . . 3 . . . 4 . . . 5 . . .—until one day you do the same thing, and I explode and erupt like an emotional volcano. You don't understand, and rightfully feel that my reaction was totally out of place. You are hurt and bruised. Our relationship is damaged—all because I didn't share with you the first time how that one thing you do bothers me. Not wishing to hurt you over a little thing, I let it fester until I hurt you worse. Wanting things peaceful, I created a whirlwind. That was repression, then eruption.

Every time we are angry and repress it, we store tension in our muscles, stress in our stomachs or respiratory systems, and set the stage for psychosomatic illnesses. Sometimes we cope with anger by indirect expression such as nagging, whining, and harping, or we maliciously gossip about someone we are afraid to confront directly.

Sometimes we displace our anger by taking it out on someone more vulnerable than we are; for example, kicking the dog or screaming at our spouse, when we are really angry at our boss. Sometimes we turn our anger inward causing depression and self-resentment. Repression directly or indirectly is unhealthy.

Control of our emotions differs from repression. Control recognizes the emotion and owns it: "*I* am angry." It is a recognition that we have chosen to react in a certain way and does not blame the other person. Control never says, "*You* make me angry."

Control then deals with the unwanted emotion. Sometimes we can deal with emotion by changing our thinking and attitudes when we talk to ourselves. Then in truth the problem is gone. The emotion is released. Consider the retirement syndrome, for example. Viewing retirement as a punishment for growing old produces unhealthy feelings. Viewing retirement as a reward for a lifetime of work releases those feelings.

At other times we can control emotion by being honest with the source of our reaction. To illustrate: "Perhaps I shouldn't let this bother me in light of your working schedule, and I don't wish to imply that you are at fault, but I get upset when you don't telephone, telling me you'll be late." If we cannot release the emotion, then we can channel it into some constructive goal.

(5) Emotional Outbursts

Even more difficult, sometimes, is dealing with people who cannot control their emotions. If someone explodes at you, stay calm. Some of these people are masters of escalated conflict. Be firm but do not react in kind, tit for tat. Use defusing statements like . . .

"I see that you are upset."

"You obviously feel strongly about this topic."

"In my opinion . . ."

"It is my judgment that . . ."

"I'm sorry I forgot . . ."

Then just let the person blow off steam until he is calm. If you have remained calm, he will probably apologize for his tirade. If you feel that you cannot remain calm, leave the room, agreeing to discuss the matter in a more tranquil atmosphere. If someone should burst into tears, simply wait until the crying is over. If it persists, agree to discuss the matter later.

At any rate, sharing our emotions, even at the surface level, involves a deeper level of trust than that required for casual conversation. Our emotional competence is put on the line! The Bible says, "A man without self-control is like a city broken into and left without walls" (Proverbs 25:28).

d. The Intellectual Level. A fourth and deeper level of communication is reached when we share ideas. Here we risk acceptance of our ideas and of ourselves. We are ego-involved with our ideas, proposals, and projects. If our serious ideas are rejected, our self-esteem is often threatened. If our proposals are praised, our self-concept soars like an eagle. Our risk-taking regarding ideas is dependent upon our self-confidence and self-esteem.

Perhaps the most important cause of a person's success or failure, in work or in personal relationships, is what he believes about himself. There is no value judgment more crucial, no variable more decisive in his personality development or in his motivation, than the estimate he places on himself. The person who has had success can take risks more freely because his self-confidence can afford it. This is why success is so important to motivation. A person with a history of failure is reluctant to risk failure again.

In every exchange of ideas we risk judgment, error, disapproval, censure, and rejection. At a deeper level we risk our self-concept. Mutual trust and acceptance build up our confidence giving us a surplus to risk—making us feel good about ourselves, unlocking the door to success.

e. The Peak Level. This is the highest level of communication. To reach this level a great amount of trust is required.

Each of us has a public self—aspects of our personalities that we want others to see. We don different masks according to the face we feel we should present in different situations. Each social role has its own mask of expected behaviors.

Many times our masks are projections of our ideal self—the person we would really like to be. Sometimes our masks are shields to hide feelings we do not wish to reveal—defense mechanisms to protect ourselves. Then sometimes our masks hide aspects of our personalities from our own awareness.

Our self-image is the picture we have of ourselves. It is never totally accurate, for we never see ourselves as God sees us. We are never totally aware of our personality, needs, and wants, for part of us is the unconscious where we are blind to our impulses, wishes, and repressed memories. Sometimes our self-image is distorted, making us oblivious to our potentiality and capability. An optimist makes perhaps as many mistakes as a pessimist. The big difference is that the optimist has more fun. The optimistic minister believes that he pastors the best of all churches. The pessimistic minister fears that this is true.

Our self-concept may be distinguished from our self-image as a constellation of attitudes we hold about our worth as a person. It is the value we place on ourselves. Our self-concept develops from a comparison of our self-image with our ideal self. If our ideal self is unrealistically high for our stage of Christian progress and maturity, we may be plagued with guilt, depression, negative self-esteem, and self-disparagement.

Almost every Christian worker recognizes and is sensitive to a crippling handicap. Negative self-esteem is usually more debilitating and crippling, yet is overlooked because we fail to take the time to establish a relationship of mutual trust where we can become sensitive to another's self-image—the way a child or adult sees himself and his abilities.

Our real self is the self God sees, our authentic core. It is a contradictory self—sometimes one part wars against another. It is a large self, encompassing our entire past and present, both conscious and unconscious. It is a multitudinous and crowded self wearing many hats, starring in many roles, divided in many parts each striving for attention and dominance, yet searching for coherence and longing for harmony. It is a dynamic, changing self. Like Alice in Wonderland, we sometimes can say, "I know who I was when I got up this morning, but I think I must have changed several times since then."[12]

Originated by Dr. Eric Berne, and popularized by Dr. Thomas Harris in the book *I'm OK—You're OK*,

---

[12] Alice, responding to Caterpillar's question, "Who are you?" *Alice's Adventures in Wonderland* by Lewis Carroll (pen name of Charles Dodgson, 1832-1898).

transactional analysis identifies three selves that appear to be present in all of us. These selves are the Parent, the Adult, and the Child. A *transaction* may be defined briefly as "an isolated unit of social interchange in which I speak to you and you respond by speaking to me." We then analyze each unit of interaction to see which one of our selves was communicating—Parent, Adult, or Child.

The Parent refers to that part of us, that collection of data, gathered in the first five years of infancy in which our parents or guardians were the dominant influence in our lives. The Parent includes all the prohibitions, admonitions, rules, and laws that we as a child accepted unquestionably from our parents and saw in their living. It also includes all the pleasures we shared with our parents, including their warmth and expression of affection. The Parent stays with us throughout life and is most influential and clearly seen when we attempt to coerce, force, threaten, command, restrict, or control our children or another person. The Parent is the self in control when we speak dogmatically, conveying the weight of indisputable authority. It is also the self in control when we judge, find fault, and blame others. Sometimes, however, the Parent is permissive and indulgent.

The Child in us is the recording of all our internal responses, our feelings that we had as a child in response to our parents, siblings, and environment. Much in the Child is negative. Helpless and dependent, we viewed ourselves as clumsy, stupid, inept, or not OK. As a child, we were controlled by our feelings. Emotion dominated reason. So as an adult, when feelings dominate reason, we say the Child is the self in control. On the positive side, the Child inspires creativity, curiosity, exploration, and sensitivity.

The Adult is a continuous data-processing computer that makes decisions after gathering and weighing all the available evidence. The Adult in us adjusts to new data and makes any necessary changes. It generates solutions to problems. It estimates the probable outcome of various choices. The Adult does not ignore feelings (the Child), but lets reason rule. When we are open-minded, logical, and reasonable, the Adult is the self in control.

Transactional analysis exposes the communicative games we play. Sometimes the games are harmless, such as the operation game described earlier. Sometimes they are devastatingly enervating, such as the "yes, but . . ." game. This is a game of negation and defeat. To every positive suggestion the player of this game says "yes, but . . ." and then gives one hundred reasons why that suggestion won't work for him. We all know players of this game. Mutual trust helps us identify the games we play, ridding ourselves of the harmful ones.

Transactional analysis also constructs four possible responses to ourselves and to others:

1. I'm not OK—you're OK.
2. I'm not OK—you're not OK.
3. I'm OK—you're not OK.
4. I'm OK—you're OK.[13]

Only one of these, "I'm OK—you're OK," makes for a healthy communicative relationship. The peak level of

---

[13] Thomas A. Harris, *I'm OK—You're OK* (New York: Avon Books, 1973), Chapter IV, pp. 60-77. (Originally copyrighted in 1967 and published by Harper and Row.)

communication is achieved only in an atmosphere of complete trust. It is the real you, with all your parts—Parent, Child, and Adult—conversing intimately, stripped of all masks and games. It is communicating not just trifles, but things that really matter—sharing, caring, disclosing who you are and where you are.

John Powell has written an excellent little book, *Why Am I Afraid to Tell You Who I Am?*[14] The answer? Lack of trust. Fear of being unloved and unaccepted. Fear of being ridiculed and teased. Trust banishes this fear of disclosure, enabling us to say with H. C. Lyon, Jr., in the title of his book, *It's Me and I'm Here*.[15] Trust provides the climate for peak communication, allowing self-realization in the process of disclosure. We most clearly see ourselves through the genuine communication of reciprocal trust and acceptance.

Toward the end of his long and productive life of 86 years, Carl Jung wrote a short but significant book, *The Undiscovered Self*. Here the Swiss psychiatrist pled for a "whole-souled" encounter in which the resources of two persons are openly engaged, without artificial role-playing or defensive disguises. Synthesis, wholeness, and the dynamic organization of personality, creative potential, self-realization, and becoming are achieved, most readily, Jung says, through empathic, communicative encounter.

---

[14] John Powell, *Why Am I Afraid to Tell You Who I Am?* (Niles, Ill.: Argus Communications, 1969).

[15] H. C. Lyon, Jr., *It's Me and I'm Here* (New York: Delacorte Press, 1974).

The Protestant Theologian Paul Tillich, in his most popular book, *The Courage to Be*, called this affiliation with others a daring act of self-affirmation. Emptiness, hollowness, loneliness even in a crowd, and self-alienation where one's own feelings seem foreign—"I'm not myself today" or "I can't imagine why I did that"—all this malaise can be changed by trusting encounters with others and with God, "the Ground of Being," if we have the courage to be ourselves.[16]

Catholic Theologian Gabriel Marcel, in *The Mystery of Being*,[17] and Jewish Theologian Martin Buber, in *I and Thou*[18], see personal awareness coming through a communicative, trusting relationship with others and with God. Both describe a true relationship with God or man as one where the other is truly met, trusted, and addressed. This is contrasted by an "I-it" relationship where God or persons are reduced to objects and treated as tools or conveniences.

Let us elaborate on a tremendous truth here. If a husband perceives or treats his wife as an object, a machine who cooks and washes clothes or performs in any other role—or if a wife treats her husband as a machine that brings home money and mows the lawn or performs in any other role, the relationship is

---

[16] Paul Tillich, *The Courage to Be* (New Haven, Conn.: Yale University Press, 1952), p. 3. The concept is also developed in *Systematic Theology*, 3 vols. (1951-1963), Part II.

[17] Gabriel Marcel, *The Mystery of Being*, 2 vols. (1950-1951). See also his plays: *La Grace*, *Le Palais de Sable*, and *Le Coeur des Autres*.

[18] Martin Buber, *Ich Und Du (I and Thou)*, 1923.

demeaning, unfulfilling, and destructive to both. Feelings die in this kind of communicative climate. What about our relationship with God? Viewing God as an object, as a Hilton bellhop or a magic genie, misses the wonder of encounter, communication, and fellowship. Prayer is shallow when it consists of directives ("God, do this, and God, do that") or a Santa Claus list ("God, give me this, and God, give me that"). Prayer can be destructive and self-defeating when it is problem-centered rather than Person-centered. Prayer is foremost an encounter!

Dr. Harry Stack Sullivan in *The Interpersonal Theory of Psychiatry*, Dr. Carl Rogers *On Becoming a Person* and *On Personal Power*, and many others see health and self-realization coming, in large part, from trusting, interpersonal encounters.

Trust is not always easy. It often requires going the second mile to ignore another's negative characteristics and to identify the real person behind a defensive facade. Trust involves risk and, many times, hurt. Trust doesn't just happen. Someone has to begin the cycle of being trustworthy and trusting. Communication thrives on trust.

This does not mean that we should trust everyone or that we should trust everyone equally. Some persons demonstrate that they cannot be trusted. Jesus did not trust the Pharisees who conspired to entrap Him. Jesus trusted the Seventy more than the multitude, to whom He spoke in parables so that "they may not understand" (Luke 8:4, 10; 10:1). He trusted the Twelve more than the Seventy by placing on their shoulders a heavier responsibility. He trusted Peter, James, and John more than the other nine. It was just these and the parents who were permitted to witness the raising of Jairus' 12-year-old daughter (Luke 8:51). These alone were chosen to see Jesus transfigured before them when "his face shone like the sun, and his garments became white as light" (Matthew 17:1-8). Peter, James, and John alone were trusted to share Christ's agony in Gethsemane when "his sweat became like great drops of blood falling down upon the ground" (Matthew 26:36-46; Luke 22:44). Trust should be commensurate with the level of responsibility or the depth of the relationship.

LANGUAGE

Trust has its own unique language. It avoids passing judgment or placing blame on the other person. Trust is descriptive ("The work is not yet done") rather than demeaning ("You're lazy") . . . objective ("The conference was organized superbly") rather than subjective ("You're a good man, Thompson"). Praise or criticism is psychologically sound when *directed toward* the work, deed, or act and *directed away from* the character or personality.

Trust does not bait the other into defensiveness. It does not ask questions to which it knows the answers, trapping a person in half-truths. A Father does not ask, "Son, how are you doing in math?" Rather, he is forthright: "Son, your teacher called to report your low grade in math. What can I do to help?"

Trust allows the other the right to express emotions—even negative ones—without guilt or censure, understanding that they might be transient and fleeting. Trust mirrors feelings positively: "I see you are upset. You have a right to be."

Trust does not threaten: "If you do it one more time, I'll . . ." Trust expects no next time.

Trust uses language fostering growth and responsibility. A minister may reply to a seasoned staff member's question, "You decide; your past experience qualifies you. . . . Whatever you decide is all right with me."

CONCLUSION

We can learn the language of trust. Trust is descriptive rather than judgmental or blaming. Praise or criticism is directed toward the act and away from the personality. The language of trust is honest and straightforward. It does not bait or trap. Trust does not threaten. Trust uses language fostering growth and responsibility. The language of trust is assertive but not aggressive or demanding. It is never manipulative or deceptive.

Someone has to begin the cycle of trust. This may be accomplished by the following code: (1) Trust moderately even though you are not sure the other person will trust you or will prove trustworthy. (2) Never exploit or take advantage of the other's trust. And (3) as trust is rewarded by reliability and responsiveness, negotiate deeper levels of commitment and responsibility. Progressively share at deeper levels of feeling and ideas.

Trust is just one ingredient of successful communicative climate. We are ready now to examine another one, which I call love.

3

THE ELEMENT OF LOVE

Moses, the Old Testament lawgiver, equated goodness supremely with justice. Plato, the Greek philosopher, saw goodness essentially as wisdom. Jesus, the Christ, perceived goodness centrally as love.

Love is the alternate heartbeat of trust. Love begins and thrives in a climate of trust. In Chapter 1 we saw that love is a dynamic springboard of human motivation. People will do for love what they wouldn't do for any other reason. An appeal to our need to love, to be loved, and to belong is powerful and persuasive. In the context of this chapter, we are saying that love is indispensable to interpersonal relationships in general, and specifically to a communicative climate.

Today, love is the message—from psychiatry and psychology to interpersonal communication and employee relations. Dr. Leo Buscaglia teaches a course on love each semester at the University of Southern California. It has become one of the university's most popular courses. Buscaglia also lectures on college campuses across the country calling the learning of love the most important preparation for life. Courses like economics and math are important, but not essential. What is essential is love and that can be learned at any age.[1]

For the most part, these academic cries for love come from a non-Christian context. Some, like Eric Fromm, for instance, disavow any belief in God. Yet these voices have one thing in common. They all express an idea that is the title of one of the first books by a psychiatrist on the subject: Dr. Smiley Blanton's book *Love or Perish*.[2] Without love people die, relationships die, groups and organizations die, churches die, in part because without love communication dies.

Without love there is both dis-ease and disease, the stunted growth of personality and psyche. Love fosters health, beauty, and human potential. Love unblocks the channels through which creativity and inspiration flow. Love is a pacemaker to the heart of group growth. From it stem all other significant variables of health, which nourish the entire organizational system.

Hospitalized infants respond quicker to treatment when held regularly by nurses. Some apparently die from no other cause than lack of affection. Hospital patients of all ages tend to recover sooner if the attending physician shows some warmth, such as holding their hands.[3] A physician told me, "I can tell

---

[1] F. Leonardo Buscaglia, a video-taped lecture at the University of Wisconsin, Eau Claire, "What Is Essential Is Invisible to the Eye," October 14, 1975.

[2] Smiley Blanton, *Love or Perish* (New York: Simon and Schuster, 1956).

[3] Harry Stack Sullivan, *The Interpersonal Theory of Psychiatry* (New York: Norton, 1953).

what is wrong with a patient through various tests, but I take time to listen because caring is vital to the healing process."

When we turn to the educational process, the same story emerges. By and large, we learn most from those we love. As the Poet Gibran puts it: "The teacher gives not of his wisdom, but rather of his faith and lovingness."[4] Learning is something the student does for himself when the climate for learning has been established. If facts are the seeds that later produce knowledge and wisdom, then love is the fertile soil in which those seeds can grow.

Both children and adults need to experience success and competence to build a self-concept of worth. But each person needs to feel loved regardless of his competence. Successful performances in the classroom or on the job give a sense of personal worth. Being cherished as a person gives the feeling of being loved. Every person needs to feel both loved and worthwhile. But lovability must never be tied to performance. The amazing thing is this: the more we make anyone feel loved, the more likely he will perform in satisfactory ways on the job or in the classroom, for then he loves himself. Hence our lives are molded by those who love us and by those who refuse to love us.

God's love for us is not dependent upon our performance or perfection. He loved the Prodigal Son as much as the Elder Brother who remained home with the Father (Luke 15:8-32). The fact that God loves the sinner shows us what kind of ultimate love it must be. It's the kind of love that won't wear thin! To see how

---

[4] Kahlil Gibran, *The Prophet* (New York: A. A. Knopf, 1976).

God in His love would act toward us, read 1 Corinthians 13:4-8.

Keith Miller has written a book entitled *Please Love Me*.[5] It is a biography about Hedy—one woman's silent plea for the miracle of intimacy. Hedy is not alone. Her plea is everyone's plea. As Leonard Nimoy of *Star Trek* fame says in his poetry: "We are all children searching for love."[6]

Obviously we are not talking about eros or sexual love, although eros is beautiful within the context of marriage. Dr. Erich Fromm's excellent book *The Art of Loving* is not a treatise on lovemaking.[7] Nor will Dr. Rollo May's book *Love and Will*[8] read like Erich Segal's *Love Story*. We are talking about love as expressed by the New Testament Greek words *agape* and *philia*. We are talking about love in terms of attitude plus action: acceptance, forgiveness, giving, caring, responsibility, respect, and knowledge. In a Christian context, these words take on added significance.

ACCEPTANCE

Love means acceptance—first of ourselves, then of others. No one can really love and accept others until he has learned to love and accept himself.

Observe the following Scripture:

> *One of the scribes . . . asked him, "Which commandment is the first of all?" Jesus answered,*

---

[5] Keith Miller, *Please Love Me* (Waco, Texas: Word Books, 1977).
[6] Leonard Nimoy, *We Are All Children Searching for Love* (Boulder, Colo.: Blue Mountain Press, 1977).
[7] Erich Fromm, *The Art of Loving* (New York: Harper and Row, 1956).
[8] Rollo May, *Love and Will* (New York: W. W. Norton and Co., 1969).

> "The first is, 'Hear, O Israel: The Lord our God, the Lord is one; and you shall love the Lord your God with all your heart, and with all your soul, and with all your mind, and with all your strength.' The second is this, 'You shall love your neighbor as yourself.' There is no other commandment greater than these." And the scribe said to him, "You are right, Teacher; you have truly said that he is one, and there is no other but he; and to love him with all the heart, and with all the understanding, and with all the strength, and to love one's neighbor as oneself, is much more than all whole burnt offerings and sacrifices." And when Jesus saw that he answered wisely, he said to him, "You are not far from the kingdom of God" (Mark 12:28-34).

Notice first, that to love God supremely and to love one's neighbor as oneself is more important than the entire Old Testament system of burnt offerings and sacrifices (cf. 1 Samuel 15:22). As early as the seventh century B.C. the Prophet Jeremiah had placed the sacrificial system in similar perspective (Jeremiah 7:21-23). In the same spirit, we may say today that to love God and neighbor is more important than venerating the Cross.

Love is always more important than its symbol. To love God and neighbor is more important than Scripture, doctrine, denomination, litany, liturgy, prayer, tithe, offerings, tongues, miracles, prophecy, preaching, Eucharist, baptism, confirmation, Lent, Ash Wednesday, Good Friday, Easter Sunday, Ascension, Pentecost or Christmas!

Notice, second, that we are to love our neighbor as ourselves. In this command, Jesus forever destroyed the myth that self-love is wrong, selfish, or undesirable. To the contrary, the more we love ourselves, the more we can love others. The person who does not love himself spends so much energy reaching out to others for love that he has little to give in return. He resembles a man with a severe toothache; that is, he can think only about his own pain.

Writings that deprecate man, such as the two-volume *Nature and Destiny of Man* by Theologian Reinhold Niebuhr, miss the mark. Songs that deprecate us should be revised or expunged from our hymnals, We are not a "worm" as one hymn describes us. The song "I am unworthy, the least of his favor" fails to grasp the meaning of God's love, which says one person is worth more than the entire world! The Bible says, "See what love the Father has given us, that we should be called children of God; and so we are. . . . Beloved, we are God's children now; it does not yet appear what we shall be, but we know that when he appears we shall be like him, for we shall see him as he is" (1 John 3:1, 2).

To be sure, one should not be inflated with conceit or vanity, a condition of excessive pride in one's appearance or accomplishments. Humility characterizes the mature and realistic personality. However, when we hear the braggart, intoxicated with the exuberance of his own verbosity, boasting of his exploits, we are probably not hearing from a man with a sense of great self-worth. We are probably not hearing from a man who loves himself too much. Most likely, we are hearing just the opposite. We are hearing psychologically a man who doubts his own worth, who feels inferior, who feels inadequate, and who is crying for recognition.

Conversely, the one who deprecates himself is rarely humble. Self-condemnation often is a cloak for pride and arrogance. The person is really saying: "Look how great I am. I have such lofty standards and ideals that I am utterly ashamed of myself when I fall even a wee bit short." Spinoza, the seventeenth-century Dutch philosopher, captured psychological and scriptural truth when he said: "One who despises himself is the nearest to a proud man." In the Golden Age of Democracy in ancient Athens, politicians wore tattered garments in an effort to appear humble and thus win the vote of the poor. Socrates unmasked this hypocrisy: "Your vanity shows forth from every hole in your coat."[9]

The loving person accepts himself as a Christian in process. He is aware of his good points from natural talents to cultivated virtues. He is also aware of his imperfections and limitations. He accepts these shortcomings for the present as part of being human—as a starting place for spiritual growth. He sets goals for continued improvement, but is gentle with himself if he stumbles and fails. He sees himself as God sees him.

Loving yourself is the key to victory over feelings of depression. Depression, a complex destructive emotion, often has its root in the lack of self-love and self-esteem. Depression mushrooms when we judge ourselves unlovable, unworthy, or unacceptable. Acceptance of oneself must never be tied to performance. God does not bestow His love on the basis of our performance, and neither should we.

---

[9] For a much more complete discussion of self-love versus pride, see Rollo May, *Man's Search for Himself* (New York: W. W. Norton and Co., 1953), Chapter 3, "The Experience."

Loving yourself is the key to victory over unfounded jealousy. Unwarranted jealousy is a negative emotion that swells within us when we see ourselves as unlovable to our mate or friends, while picturing others as lovable. It's the "I'm not OK—you're OK" problem discussed earlier.

Loving yourself is the key to victory over gossip and stinging, negative criticism of others. We tend to tear others down in an unconscious effort to make ourselves look good. When we love ourselves sufficiently, we have no need to make others look or feel bad!

Self-acceptance or self-love is essential to victory over anger and temper. Much of our irritability, irascibility, and anger come from a dissatisfaction with ourselves. We strike out at others because we are warring with ourselves. Self-love brings inward peace and, consequently, warmth to others.

Therefore, love yourself. Accept yourself. You're unique in all the world. Dr. Bruce Narramore has written an excellent book: *You're Someone Special*.[10] And you *are* special. Paint a beautiful picture of yourself and walk into it. You are the best "you" that anyone could be. No one else could be a better "you." Most important, you are special to God and that's being really special.

The loving person accepts others. He realizes that everyone comes with pluses and minuses. He focuses on the strong points and overlooks the weak points. Everyone has beauty, but only the loving person sees

---

[10] Bruce Narramore, *You're Someone Special* (Grand Rapids, Michigan: Zondervan, 1978).

it. Will Rogers understood this when he said, "I have never met a man I didn't like."

Even a dog can tell if he is wanted and accepted. People are much more intuitive than dogs and can determine quickly if they are accepted. In many subtle and unconscious ways—by gesture, tone, syntax, pause, and attitude—we signal acceptance or rejection of others. Everyone secretly searches for a yes that tells him he is affirmed in his being by another. Love is that yes of acceptance, the semaphore of communication. When we send rejection signals, we block communication.

At least two situations present a problem of acceptance: (1) the expression of an unacceptable idea, and (2) the performance of an unacceptable act. A good communicative climate is one where the person is totally accepted even though his ideas or his actions are not.

1. We have difficulty accepting others if their ideas are incompatible with ours. The more emotionally involved we are with the topic of discussion, the more we tend to direct our rejection and hostility toward the person. "You are not only wrong, you are stupid," we say attitudinally if not verbally.

2. This tendency is even more pronounced when we observe unacceptable behavior. We see the person as bad and as unacceptable as his behavior. This is, of course, the spirit of the Pharisee, and not the Spirit of Christ. The religious leaders of His day were appalled that Jesus would have dinner with a chief tax collector like Zacchaeus, who assessed tribute for Rome, an oppressive foreign government—and on a commission basis (Luke 19:2-10)! The Pharisees were horrified that Jesus would even speak to a prostitute.

Yet He not only talked to one, but allowed her to wash His feet with her tears and dry them with her hair—to kiss His feet and soothe them with expensive oil. You see, the Pharisees saw her as dirt and trash. Jesus saw her as special: "Therefore I tell you, her sins, which are many, are forgiven, for she loved much; but he who is forgiven little, loves little" (Luke 7:36-50). Jesus was able to separate an unacceptable act from an acceptable person.

If "Christ Jesus came into the world to save sinners" (1 Timothy 1:15), if the Father indeed rejoices more over one sinner who returns to the fold than 99 "that never went astray" (Matthew 18:13), if the Father's arms are forever open to receive the prodigal, if God's kitchen operates 24 hours a day to serve the fatted calf to the wayward (Luke 15:11-32), how can we as His ambassadors reject people?

How can a person feel loved unless somebody loves him? How can a person feel wanted unless somebody wants him? How can a person feel accepted unless somebody accepts him? How can an individual feel personal dignity and integrity unless somebody treats him so? Our arms are the only arms God has chosen to use. If people are going to see that God accepts them, they must first see that acceptance in us!

Two tactics are helpful here. First, separate the idea of an individual from the person himself. Brilliant men sometimes express illogical ideas or offer foolish suggestions. The Bible says, "Great men are not always wise" (Job 32:9, KJV). It is the idea or suggestion that is illogical or foolish, rather than the person. The person is not wrong. He is simply expressing what he thinks or believes at the time. And nothing is wrong about being honest, different, or being oneself. To the person, show confirmation of listening. To the person, show acceptance. Affirmation and acceptance can be demonstrated by sincere responses such as nodding affirmatively and saying . . .

"I hear what you are saying."

"I see where you are coming from."

"It is obvious that this problem concerns you deeply."

Affirmation and acceptance of the person does not mean acceptance of the idea:

"I am pleased that you have given a great deal of thought to this subject."

"May I share with you where I am at this time?"

"Several things trouble me about this issue."

So, the first tactic in achieving the goal of accepting others is to separate an unacceptable idea from an acceptable person. We can always demonstrate confirmation of listening and total acceptance of the person even though we must reject part or all of a person's idea. Accept the person, and the next time he has an idea, he will feel free to share it with you. Reject the person, however, and you will have stymied further ideas—ideas that you and your organization may vitally need.

The second tactic in achieving the goal of accepting others is to separate unacceptable behavior from an acceptable person. As you may know, this is a sound principle of child psychology.

There are times when little Johnny behaves in an unacceptable way. The parents properly reject the act: "We see you have written on the wall. Writing on the wall is not permitted in this house. Your paper is meant for writing with pencils. Your blackboard is given for writing with chalk. Your coloring book is made for writing with crayons. Walls are never meant for writing."

At the same time, Johnny is loved dearly by his parents. That love through acceptance must be shown clearly if Johnny is to grow up healthy, free from emotional scars. If punishment of any kind becomes necessary, it is even more important that the child feel acceptance of his person.

Notice the principles of communication illustrated in the correction of Johnny. First, the parents control their feelings. There is no emotional tirade, no long vituperative speech censoring or denouncing the child.

Second, the parents use no invective of abuse or insult, no attack on the person. The child is not called "stupid, arrogant, bad, naughty, rebellious, terrible, obnoxious, or no-good." To do so is to commit perhaps the most deadly of all sins—the mutilation of a child's spirit. The Bible says, "Fathers, provoke not your children to anger, lest they be discouraged" (Colossians 3:21, KJV; see also Ephesians 6:4).

Third, the parents speak to the problem: "I see you have written on the wall. Writing on the wall is not permitted." Positive statements are made as to where writing is permitted. Then appropriate punishment is administered as a consequence of his inappropriate action. If the child is old enough, and if the surface is washable, the child should be expected to clean the walls. Acceptance of the child is evident at all times in spite of any punitive measures.

The same communicative principles are effective in dealing with an adult. Suppose a worker through carelessness breaks a machine vital to production. The skilled foreman remains in emotional control. He does not attack the person of the employee. He does not say, "You clumsy idiot, how can you be so careless?" Rather, he speaks to the problem that is costing the company money by lost productivity. His first concern is the employee: "Are you hurt? I'm glad you're OK." Then the foreman considers the machine: "I'll get a maintenance man here right away." Speaking to the problem avoids confrontation and a potential grievance complaint. It increases communicative effectiveness. It decreases downtime while providing a positive climate for future work.

Turning to a church setting, a Sunday school superintendent regularly may berate those who are present for those who are absent. In private the minister of education may discuss the problem while showing warm acceptance of the superintendent as a person, and appreciation for his service. Similarly, a superintendent may address the problem of noise in a teacher's classroom. Perhaps she needs a teacher's aide. Perhaps the class is too large. Several suggestions may be offered for increased teacher effectiveness. But the problem is addressed, not the person. It can only hurt the cause of Christ to attack the teacher's incompetency, inability, or style of presentation. The teacher always must feel accepted and part of the church team. How many can you recall over the years who were hurt or, even worse, sidelined because some church leader did not know these principles of communication?

Enlist each one in your church to try this experiment. For 30 days treat everyone you meet, in or out of the church, with total acceptance regardless of his ideas or behavior. View the troublemaker as a worthwhile person needing recognition. View the gossip as a person needing self-esteem. View the boaster as a person suffering from feelings of inferiority and inadequacy. View the jealous person as a person needing to feel loved. View the tyrant as a person throwing the weight of his authority around because he craves a little respect. View the ill-tempered person as but at war with himself. View the person loose with the truth as but suffering from defensiveness such as denial, rationalization, or projection. View the drunkard as but suffering from the bonds of alcoholism. Try overlooking everyone's faults, including those of your mate. Try concentrating on everyone's virtues including your own.

Do this for 30 days. You will like the results. You will be surprised how much more you are accepted. You will discover the truth of Jesus' words: "Judge not, and you will not be judged; condemn not, and you will not be condemned" (Luke 6:37; see also Matthew 7:1). You will be surprised how much easier it is to talk to people. A new productive communication climate will emerge. You will like the change in yourself and others so much that you will want to live the rest of your life with an attitude of acceptance.

Over a period of time, a continuous and steadfast focus on the positive in life, on our strengths and the strengths of others, will give us and our followers a sense of worth and power. By accepting others, we help them to see themselves as a positive force. They then will contribute to the task of building a better church, a better organization, a better community, and a better world.

FORGIVENESS

To love is to forgive. If we are to love ourselves, we must forgive ourselves. If we are to love our brothers and sisters in Christ, we must forgive one another. If we are to love our neighbors, we must forgive our neighbors. If we are to love our enemies, we must forgive our enemies.

What does forgiveness mean? To forgive means to pardon with compassion on a directly personal level, to free a person from the consequences of his guilt, or sometimes to pass over a blameworthy action without censure or punishment. Most of all, to forgive means to rid *ourselves* completely of all resentment, indignation, hostility, anger, or ill will felt as a result of a real or imagined offense.

Of the 70 parables and similes of Jesus recorded for us in the New Testament, one story is remembered for both its hyperbole and its teaching on the subject of forgiveness. It is the Parable of the Unmerciful Servant (Matthew 18:21-35).

Jesus told this parable in response to Peter's question: "Lord, how often shall my brother sin against me, and I forgive him? As many as seven times?"

Jesus replied, "I do not say to you seven times, but seventy times seven." To explain to the puzzled apostle why he should forgive anyone 490 times, or indefinitely, Jesus taught the basis of forgiveness for all Christians with the following illustration.

A king decided to settle accounts with his servants. Jesus hyperbolized that one servant owed the monarch the stupendous sum of 10,000 talents. Jesus did not specify whether He meant a talent of gold or silver.[11] The Hebrew talent was the largest unit of weight measuring 93 pounds, 12 ounces avoirdupois, or 1,500 ounces. So Jesus was saying that this servant owed the astronomical sum of millions in silver or billions in gold!

Since the servant obviously could not pay, the king decreed that the servant, along with his wife and children, should be sold into slavery, and that all his possessions should be confiscated. Caught in this dilemma, the servant fell on his knees and implored the king for mercy. Moved with compassion, the king remitted the entire debt.

But that same servant, who was forgiven a debt of billions of dollars, decided to call in an account with a man who owed him a mere 100 denarii—less than $20. Despite a similar entreaty for mercy and an extension of time, this creditor callously threw his helpless debtor into prison.

When the story was related to the king, he summoned the culprit and said: "You wicked servant! I forgave you all that debt because you besought me; and should not you have had mercy on your fellow servant, as I had mercy on you?" And in retribution, the king delivered him to the "torturers."

Jesus closed the story with a stern moral: "So also my heavenly Father will do to every one of you, if you do not forgive your brother from your heart."

Just as the miracles of Jesus are parables of teach-

---

[11] A talent was used to measure metals. When referring to money, it usually meant gold (1 Kings 9:14; 10:10, etc.) or silver (2 Kings 5:22); but it was also used with lead (Zechariah 5:7), bronze (Exodus 38:29), or iron (1 Chronicles 29:7).

ing, the parables of Jesus are miracles of teaching. Jesus was saying that each of us, like the man in the parable, owed the inconceivable sum of billions of dollars to God, our creditor. We could never pay; but God, out of a love beyond our comprehension, forgave the entire amount. By comparison, any debt owed us is trivial. How can we Christians, who have been forgiven so much, refuse forgiveness to others? Indeed, we cannot!

The person who does not forgive is sentenced to the "torturers." This is true, not because God arbitrarily decrees it so. It is true because unforgiveness endogenously produces torment. Just as with hate, unforgiveness destroys us like a cancer. It gnaws at our vitals sometimes physically as well as psychologically.

First, forgive yourself. When you think about your life, do you feel that you have fouled up many of your closest relationships? that much you have touched seems to have gone wrong? that you have failed the Lord so often that He must be tired of hearing your confession? Or is there one main thing of the past that haunts you?

Forgive yourself completely. The negative, unproductive, crippling emotion of guilt has absolutely no place in the life of a Christian. Until you forgive yourself, you certainly will doubt your virtues and assets. It is only as you forgive yourself that you gain the sensitivity necessary to forgive others.

See yourself as God sees you. Regard your confessed past, your sin and shortcomings, as God regards them. And how does God regard them? Let us turn to the Bible and see.

Sing, O heavens, for the Lord has done it;
Shout, O depths of the earth;
Break forth into singing, O mountains,
O forest, and every tree in it (Isaiah 44:23)!

Why?

"I have swept away your transgressions like a cloud, and your sins like mist . . . for I have redeemed you" (Isaiah 44:22).

"As far as the east is from the west, so far does he move our transgressions from us" (Psalm 103:12).

How far is the east from the west? It is so far that our scientists have not been able to measure it. Our Milky Way alone, in which our sun is just one of over 100 billion stars, is approximately 100,000 light years across. A light year is the distance light travels in one year at the speed of 186,282 miles per second, or a distance of about 5.878 trillion miles. The distance across our Milky Way is 100,000 times 5.878 trillion or 5.878 quadrillion miles (587,800,000,000,000,000). If we go beyond the Milky Way and consider the entire universe, we are talking about billions of light years—an incredible distance!

Other Scriptures speak of our sins as buried in the depths of the ocean (Micah 7:19), made white as snow or wool (Isaiah 1:18), washed [away] (Revelation 1:5, KJV), cast behind God's back (Isaiah 38:17), blotted out and forgotten (Isaiah 43:25; Hebrews 10:17). It is as if God had total and permanent forgetfulness when it comes to our sins: "I will remember [them] no more" (Hebrews 8:12). Of this we can always be sure: "If we confess our sins, he is faithful and just, and will forgive our sins and cleanse us from all unrighteousness" (1 John 1:9).

Forgive yourself. God has. Proclaim with the Apostle

Paul: "Forgetting what lies behind and straining forward to what lies ahead, I press on toward the goal for the prize of the upward call of God in Christ Jesus" (Philippians 3:13, 14).

Forgive those close to you. Sons and daughters, forgive your parents. No parent, unless psychotic, deliberately plans to hurt his children. Your parents reared you the best they knew how using a combination of styles learned, by and large, from their parents.

Of course, your parents were sometimes inconsistent, vacillating from one course of action or opinion to another. Of course, you recall pockets of hypocrisy where their lives did not equal the high standards voiced by their ideal selves. Sure, they passed on to you, consciously and unconsciously, some of their phobias, insecurities, unhealthy defense mechanisms, game-playing, and personality problems.

But remember that your parents gave to you from their treasure of blessings as well. Forgive them completely—for being human. If you are still fortunate enough to have them, discover the improved communication that comes with a climate of forgiveness.

Parents, forgive your children. Of course, they sometimes rejected your bridle, shaking off your headstall, spitting out your bit, and breaking your reins, when you from experience might have guided them safely past danger. Of course, they occasionally scoffed at your hallowed traditions, adopting new ideas and practices. Yes, they learned early how to play you one against the other. To be sure, they went through the stage where they knew it all and you knew so little.

Forgive your children completely—for being human. Accept and love them for who they are, forgetting what you wanted them to be. Remember how proud they have made you in so many ways. Discover a new ability to communicate with your children when you establish a climate of forgiveness.

Extend this forgiveness to every relationship at church. In the Sermon on the Mount, Jesus taught that forgiveness should precede worship. If you know that a member has something against you, "first be reconciled to your brother," then continue your worship (Matthew 5:24). Even if it is not you who holds the grudge, and even if you have done nothing worth an offense, Jesus said to ask for forgiveness and reconciliation anyway.

Extend this forgiveness to every relationship at work —to your superiors, to your peers, and to your subordinates. Make it a practice to remember kindnesses and virtues while forgetting offenses. It is relatively easy to forgive someone who asks for forgiveness. It is much more difficult to forgive the person blind to his offense. Remember that his ego defense mechanism has rationalized and justified his action to his own satisfaction. He has convinced himself that he has done no wrong. So forgive even when not asked. You will be amazed how easy it is to communicate in the climate of forgiveness.

Forgive those who dislike you. Extend this forgiveness even to your enemies. While hanging on the cross, Jesus prayed, "Father, forgive them; for they know not what they do" (Luke 23:34). While being stoned to death for his preaching, Stephen followed the example of Jesus: "Lord, do not hold this sin against them" (Acts 7:60).

Why did Jesus tell us to forgive even our enemies, to do good to those who hate us, to bless those who curse us, and to pray for those who abuse us (Luke

6:27, 32-37)? Not for some ulterior motive. Such motivation would fall short of the magnanimous spirit of Christ. When the Samaritans refused lodging to Jesus and His disciples, James and John wanted to "command fire to come down from heaven, and consume them, even as Elijah did" (Luke 9:54, KJV; 2 Kings 1:8-15). But Jesus taught the disciples that the spirit of Elijah was not the spirit of Christ: "For the Son of man is not come to destroy men's lives, but to save them" (Luke 9:55, 56; KJV).

Jesus taught us to forgive even our enemies because our "reward will be great," due to the principle of reciprocity: "Forgive, and you will be forgiven. . . . For the measure you give will be the measure you get back" (Luke 6:35-38). When we are forgiving, even those who dislike us tend to be forgiving. But more important, we rid ourselves of feelings that torment, conquer, and destroy us.

So forgive yourself. Forgive those close to you, 490 times a day, if necessary. Forgive even those who dislike you. Challenge your congregation or Sunday school class to refuse to take offense or hold a grudge for 30 days. Then discover a new dimension of communication in your interpersonal relationships. Love involves forgiveness.

GIVING AND CARING

We have been saying that love is a key to communicative climate, and that love means acceptance and forgiveness. Love also means giving and caring.

He is not rich who has much; rather, he is rich who gives much. The most precious gift we can offer anyone is ourselves. Love is relatively meaningless in the abstract. It is only as we give of ourselves to specific individuals that we can implement the injunction of Jesus: "A new commandment I give to you, that you love one another; even as I have loved you" (John 13:34).

One measure of a pastor's love for his congregation is the extent to which he gives of himself to his members. A teacher loves a class, by and large, to the extent that she gives of herself to her pupils. A father's love for his family is most clearly seen by how much he gives of himself to his wife, children, and parents. When Jesus was "moved with compassion" for the multitude, it resulted in the giving of Himself to the needs of individuals in that crowd.

You will recall the story of Jonah, the prophet, who preached during the reign of Jeroboam II, in the eighth century B.C. (2 Kings 14:25-27). God instructed Jonah to preach in Nineveh, the ancient capital of the Assyrian Empire. (The old city of Nineveh was discovered in the 1800's on the eastern bank of the Tigris River, across from the modern city of Mosul, in northern Iraq.)

In Nineveh Jonah pronounced impending judgment: "Yet forty days, and Nineveh shall be overthrown!" (Jonah 3:4). Apparently, Jonah had little concern for these people. They were Gentiles. Only a fish ride got him there in the first place. Once there, he hoped his message would go unheeded. When the entire population of Nineveh repented, Jonah was angry. He had hoped that God would destroy the city. Jonah showed more concern for a plant that gave him shade than he did for the lives of precious people. For Jonah, being a missionary was an undesirable job. There was no compassion, no caring, no better relations between

Assyria and Israel. The cold war continued, resulting later in the destruction of Israel.

One of the greatest lessons on caring is found in the Gospel story of the man with congenital blindness. The narrative gives us three views of the blind man: (1) through the eyes of neighbors, (2) through the eyes of the 12 apostles, and (3) through the eyes of Jesus.

How did the neighbors see him? To them, he was a beggar and nothing more. What were his dreams? What was he really like? Was he kind, pleasant, jovial? Hear the question of his neighbors: "Is not this the man who used to sit and beg?" (John 9:8). They never cared enough to look beyond the surface. He was an undesirable, stereotyped by his bothersome cry to all passers-by: "Alms for the poor."

How did the apostles see him? To them he was merely the starting point for a theological discussion. "Who sinned, this man or his parents, that he was born blind?" they asked Jesus (John 9:2). Their inquiry resembled a coroner's at an autopsy. There was no thought regarding life, goals, and dreams; they were conducting an inquest to determine the cause of death. The beggar was simply Exhibit A to satisfy curiosity: Did the sin of his parents cause the disease? Or was the blindness the punishment for evil in a previous life—metempsychosis or reincarnation, perhaps?

The view through the eyes of Jesus was different. As He passed by, "he saw a man" (John 9:1). He saw a person worthy of compassion and time. He saw a person who, despite an appearance to the contrary, was full of potential and exciting possibilities. Jesus saw a man who could believe for a miracle! Jesus saw a man worth more than the whole world. Jesus cared.

Caring implies responsibility. Jonah felt no responsibility toward Gentiles. They were pagans, heathen, dogs, and enemies—nothing more. Cain, covering up for fratricide upon God's inquiry about Abel, contemptuously asked, "Am I my brother's keeper?" (Genesis 4:9).

Just as a mother's caring results in responsibility for the needs of her child, so a Christian's caring produces a responsibility for the spiritual, emotional, and physical needs of others. A church that cares develops a wide variety of ministries to meet human need. One such ministry would be that of counseling with a staff of Christian professionals. As Christians who care, we learn to give as well as receive. We learn to go beyond the realm of our own selves in all of our relationships.

People do not care how much we know; but they do know how much we care. One reason why prayer can be so rewarding is the certain knowledge that God always cares.

RESPECT

One day, the various parts of the body engaged in an acrimonious argument over who was the greatest —not unlike the sons of Zebedee on one occasion (Mark 10:35-45; Matthew 20:20-28). Many parts such as the brain, heart, lungs, kidneys, and eyes made excellent cases for their supremacy. In a two-hour speech, the brain claimed to be the master organ of the body:

I am more wonderful than any machine ever built. From the eyes, ears, nose, mouth, and skin

I receive messages that let us experience the world around us. I control the important life processes including hunger and thirst. Even if the eye wants to blink, the muscles in the eyelids must first get their signal from me. I am the source of all emotions such as love or hate. All information storage, memory, thinking, reasoning, creativity, and speaking depend on me . . .

The heart pointed out that if he did not pump blood to the carotid arteries, the brain would suffer permanent damage in a matter of minutes. The lungs noted that the blood would be worthless without their function of supplying oxygen and removing carbon dioxide. The kidneys explained to all that they had to filter other impurities from the blood to keep the body alive. And continuing past midnight, the various organs argued seriously through advocation and rebuttal.

When, however, the intestine addressed the other organs, he was mocked with derisive laughter. Therefore, the intestine decided to teach the other parts a lesson. Despite the laxatives ingested by the mouth, and in defiance of the brain, the intestine totally shut down operations until it was respected by all!

The moral of the story is this: Whenever our communication violates the principle of respect, we store explosives in the warehouse of human trouble.

Love treats people with respect. To establish an effective climate of communication we must give others their dignity. The Reverend Jesse Jackson, Baptist minister, and director of People United to Save Humanity (PUSH), captures this concept beautifully. "Everybody is somebody," he preaches. "You may be poor, but you're somebody. You may live in a ghetto, but you're somebody." Every Christian, regardless of race, rank, or caste has inherent nobility and infinite worth.

Ten Communicative Commandments for Showing Respect

1. Respect yourself. Respect for the personality, rights, and differences of others grows out of self-respect and an appreciation for your own individuality.

2. Empathically listen and really hear what your family, friends, and associates are saying and feeling. Encourage others, especially your subordinates and children, to speak freely, openly, frequently, and with impunity.

3. Actively accept others, regardless of peculiarities, by giving adequate consideration to their ideas, suggestions, opinions, and feelings. Strive to be descriptive and nonjudgmental. Confirm that you are hearing by giving positive feedback.

4. Demonstrate a belief in the dignity of all labor however menial. Treat all your members with honor, deference, esteem, appreciation, and equality. Show the same basic respect for the custodian, who cleans your church rest room, as you would for a member of your advisory board. If both were absent for a week, whom would you miss more?

5. Invest some time in the activities and interests of your closest relationships. Move beyond the level of social amenities to the deeper level of intimacy.

6. Refuse to manipulate anyone. Refuse to use people as objects and dispensable pawns.

7. Refuse to control or smother others close to you. Provide room for freedom, learning, growth, and interdependence even with your spouse. Although you are close to each other, even as one body, you each have

your own lives and individual goals. You are always together in your hearts, but not necessarily in all activities. A healthy relationship is based on mutual development, discovery, and freedom within the spirit of Christ.

8. When criticism is necessary, address only the act or problem and never the personality.

9. Refuse to "put others down." Refuse to "put people in their place" or to give them their comeuppance. If negative reinforcement is necessary, make it a logical consequence of inappropriate action. Design all consequences to be rehabilitative and ameliorative rather than punitive and vindictive.

10. Give positive strokes whenever possible. Make others feel important. Recognize birthdays, anniversaries, and the smallest task well done. Recently I asked Allen, a third-grader, why he thought his teacher was the greatest. "She makes me feel important," he replied. That teacher has learned one of the greatest lessons in human relations.

Stroking is simply a unit of recognition. Stroking takes many forms—positive, negative, mixed, conditional, or unconditional. A positive stroke is "Your report was well-organized, interesting, and concise." A negative stroke is "You made that financial statement all wrong again." A mixed stroke is a destructive backhanded compliment: "Your sermon was inspiring—for a change." A conditional stroke is recognition given to you for your performance: "You played very well in your piano recital." An unconditional stroke is recognition for being yourself: "You are sincere, open, and free from artificial role-playing." We all need positive, conditional, and unconditional strokes to survive. Love shows respect by giving these strokes.

It is only as we respect people that we can win them to Christ. In 1628, the success of the Dutch colonies in America led the Reformed Church to send Jonas Michaelius to Christianize the Indians. After working with the American Indians in the territory that later became New York State, Michaelius wrote a letter of his experiences to his home in Holland. From the following excerpt, guess whether this missionary was successful in converting the Indians.

> *As to the natives of this country, I find them entirely savage and wild, strangers to all decency, yea, uncivil and stupid as garden snakes, proficient in all wickedness, and ungodliness, devilish men. . . . They are as thievish and treacherous as they are tall, and in cruelty they are altogether inhuman, more than barbarous. . . . How these people can best be led to the true knowledge of God . . . is hard to say. . . . I have as yet been able to discover hardly a single good point.*[12]

He further suggested in the letter that the adults were hopeless. Therefore, he thought, the children should be kidnapped from their parents and taught the way of the Lord. Undoubtedly, you guessed correctly. With such a disrespectful, condescending attitude, he got nowhere in his missionary efforts.

KNOWLEDGE

Can there be love at first sight? Occasionally a couple will tell us that, upon meeting for the first time, they instantly fell in love. Probably they are referring to the

---

[12] Jonas Michaelius, *The Annals of America*, 1493-1754 (Chicago: Encyclopedia Britannica, Inc., 1976), I, 92-94.

initial attraction of pulchritude and personality, and to the emotional thrill of genuine encounter with reciprocal interest. Perhaps that attraction grew into love without either being aware of just when the two merged.

Love, however, implies knowledge. Only as we really get to know people—how they feel and what they think—can we love them. By and large we come to know people through the content and style of their communication both verbally and nonverbally over a period of time. Love enriches communication, allowing for deeper levels of disclosure and awareness. Only as we discover each other's needs can we minister to those needs.

Through communication we come to know and understand a person's predominant life position. Knowledge of this kind is vital to hiring, motivation, and promotion.

If a person's predominant life position is "I'm OK—you're OK," he will tend to communicate willingly, openly, and straightforwardly. He will accept responsibility readily and be able to work well either by himself or in a group. He is teachable, malleable, and provisional. He handles disagreements by seeking a solution acceptable to himself and the other party. In a group, he strives for mutual consensus. He solves problems systematically and analytically. He trusts his own judgment, but is always ready to learn from the knowledge and experience of others. He is self-motivated and therefore productive. He treats his subordinates as equals. He is relatively free from game-playing, and he is easy to love. This is the kind of person we should promote or elect to a position of leadership whether in a local church or in a religious organization.

If a person's predominant life position is "I'm not OK—you're OK," the general style of his communication will be defensive and self-deprecating. He will be timid, apprehensive, hesitant, and fearful of responsibility. He will tend to be shy, shrinking from public attention. He develops slowly, needing constant reassurance and coaching. He handles disagreements by giving in, thereby often harboring deep-rooted resentment. He perceives differences in opinion as evidence of his own inadequacy. He solves problems by almost completely relying on others. He spends much of his time in overcompensating activity. He needs constant praise, warmth, and encouragement for motivation. He sees himself inferior to others. He plays victim games: "Why does this always happen to me?" "Poor me!" and "I'm stupid!" This person has great potential, which can be realized through his discovering through God's Word who he really is.

If a person's predominant life position is "I'm OK—you're not OK," his communication is both defensive and aggressive. He accepts responsibility readily but tends to be unteachable, intransigent, intractable, and dogmatic. He develops with difficulty. Learning is blocked by his know-it-all attitude. He tends to handle disagreements by blaming others and forcing them to give in to his position. He solves problems by relying on his own judgment exclusively, and by unilaterally rejecting the ideas of others. He spends time playing persecutor and blaming games, such as "Now I've got you where I want you!" making someone sorry, putting someone down, and "I told you so." He is motivated by force and higher authority. He acts superior to peers and subordinates, to spouse and family. He needs counseling, but does not realize it. He often is successful if he is the head of his own organization. He is disastrous in other positions of leadership. This person takes a special kind of love and patience, for he is his own worst enemy and does not know it.

If a person's predominant life position is "I'm not OK—you're not OK," his communication is hostile, volatile, venomous, abrupt, and poignant. This person refuses responsibility. He rarely develops without in-depth counseling and teaching. He withdraws and repeats errors on the job and in his personal life. He handles disagreement by escalating the conflict and involving a third or more parties. If a problem arises with a church member, he tries to involve half the church in the disturbance. He rarely solves problems. He succumbs to them. He plays victim, persecutor, and blaming games. He is unmotivated, but may respond to reprimands and threats if backed up by disciplinary action. His attitude toward others is one of defiance, despondency, or alienation. He sometimes keeps company with others as miserable as he. This person needs counseling, plus all the love of the Apostle John, and all the patience of Job. You cannot afford to employ this kind of person in a service organization, or give him any responsibility in a church.

CONCLUSION

We have now examined two ingredients of an effective communicative climate: trust and love. We have seen that love involves acceptance, forgiveness, caring, sharing, responsibility, respect, and knowledge. The Bible tells us that "love is of God" and that "God is love" (1 John 4:7, 8). Love is the identifying characteristic of Christians: "By this all men will know that you are my disciples, if you have love for one another" (John 13:35). "Love is patient and kind; love is not jealous or boastful; it is not arrogant or rude. Love does not insist on its own way; it is not irritable or resentful; it does not rejoice at wrong, but rejoices in the right. Love bears all things . . . endures all things. Love never ends" (1 Corinthians 13:4-8). We are now ready to examine a third ingredient of communicative climate: provisionalism.

4

THE ELEMENT OF PROVISIONALISM

The Bible says that "our knowledge is imperfect" because "now we see in a mirror dimly" (1 Corinthians 13:9, 12). History is replete with examples of the old ideas bowing before the new.

From the time of Aristotle (384-322 B.C.) to the time of Galileo (A.D. 1564-1642), people generally believed that heavy objects fell faster than light ones. It was a revolutionary idea in the late 1500s to believe, what we all know today, that all objects fall with the same acceleration unless air resistance or some other force slows them down.

From the time of Ptolemy (second century A.D.) to the time of Copernicus (A.D. 1473-1543), people believed that the earth was the center of the universe and had no motion. It was a revolutionary idea to reverse that position—so revolutionary that Galileo was forced by Pope Urban VIII in 1632 (over 100 years after the discovery) to renounce his belief in the Copernican theory to save his life! Even then he was imprisoned in his own villa in Florence for his remaining years. Of course, we all know today that Copernicus and Galileo were correct. The sun is the center of our solar system, and our earth does spin while speeding rapidly through space.

And what about today? Knowledge and information are increasing at an incredible pace. A technical library can be outdated in just six months!

Education might be described humorously as the art of specialization where the university professor learns more and more about less and less until eventually he knows everything about nothing. If the university professor tries to remain a generalist, however, he places himself in no better position. He simply learns less and less about more and more until eventually he knows nothing about everything.

A person is not just a lawyer today. He may specialize in one of at least nine areas such as corporate, criminal, or tax law. Change is so rapid that he must specialize to advise someone effectively without charging for excessive research time. A physician may be an obstetrician, pediatrician, ophthalmologist, dermatologist, podiatrist, psychiatrist, internist, anesthetist, urologist, osteopath, cardiologist, neurologist, gynecologist, otolaryngologist, hemotologist, oncologist—to name just a few! One must specialize to keep pace with new discoveries. In short, yesterday's knowledge is today's history or mythology. Information marches on!

In the relative darkness of the fourth century B.C., Socrates lit a candle enlightening the process of education through the centuries. He taught that true wisdom begins with the realization of our ignorance. On that basis, he claimed to be the wisest philosopher in Athens. He was the only teacher who knew that he did not know![1]

Put another way, our certainty increases inversely with our knowledge; that is, the more we know, the more we know that we do not know. When we increase our island of knowledge, we also increase our shoreline of mystery (see illustration). Technology is changing so rapidly that our universities must train most of its students for jobs, problems, and conditions that will not exist for another 20 years! Education must always teach contemporary knowledge. Its primary responsibility, however, is to teach students not what to think, but how to think. Our universities, therefore, must teach an approach to knowledge, how to be logical, how to research, how to be open to change, and how to keep up with new and relevant data. A childlike humility before the facts is essential—searching, questioning, exploring.

No amount of knowledge is ever ultimately contradictory to God, for God is truth. Jesus said that those who worship God "must worship in spirit and truth" (John 4:24). He also said that we "will know the truth, and the truth will make [us] free" (John 8:32) and that we should love God "with all [our] mind" (Luke 10:27; Mark 12:30). We are free, in part, to the extent that we do not fear to go to the end of our thought. The search for truth in general must never be stymied by dogmatic answers that convey the weight of undisputed authority.

---

[1] Cooper, Lane, trans., *Plato on the Trial and Death of Socrates* (Ithaca, N.Y.: Cornell University Press, 1941).

Notice how the shoreline of the unknown increases as our island of knowledge increases.

Knowledge

Shoreline of the Unknown

Knowledge

Shoreline of the Unknown

A parishioner once chided the famous nineteenth-century preacher Henry Ward Beecher that the previous year he had expressed a rather different view on the same topic. "That was last year," quipped Beecher.[2] His provisional attitude was one reason Beecher could draw an audience of 3,000 persons both Sunday morning and evening for 40 years! That is still a U.S. record. His annual salary of $100,000 from Plymouth Congregational Church of Brooklyn, New York (the equivalent of more than $1 million today), is also a record!

Provisionalism discards previous methods and thinking as quickly as yesterday's used coffee grounds—if investigation and research show a better way. The provisional person holds as his motto, "I will express what I think today although it contradicts anything I said previously—in light of new discovery." In a rapidly changing world, even equilibrium must be dynamic. One must advance just to stand still! One reason organizations like those of Billy Graham, Oral Roberts, and Pat Robertson have sustained momentum for God is the provisionalism of their leadership. Provisionalism supports a communicative climate. If a person is genuinely searching for truth and reaching for better methods, he does not resent assistance in the quest. He welcomes the ideas of others.

THE PROVISIONAL PERSON

The provisional person is open-minded, flexible, teachable, pliable, adaptable, conditional, tolerant, accepting,

---

[2] Lyman Abbott, *Life of Henry Ward Beecher* (Boston: Houghton Mifflin, 1905).

forgiving, mediating, and conciliating. The provisional person constantly seeks deeper understanding, sharper definition, clearer knowledge, more light, greater accuracy, and expanded truth. He believes that there are always better methods waiting to be discovered, and new knowledge waiting to be perceived. He sees himself and his ideas open to growth, progress, amendment, exception, experimentation, development, and change.

Provisionalism is not the enemy of conviction, belief, faith, creed, doctrine, or positive preaching. Provisionalism is not irresolute fence-straddling, pusillanimous wavering, or fainthearted indecisiveness. Provisionalism is a continual openness to all available evidence, data, and information, while acting decisively on the basis of present knowledge and experience. Provisionalism is the enemy of dogmatism, bigotry, prejudice, narrow-mindedness, conformity, stubbornness, intransigence, provincialism, intolerance, and authoritarianism. Provisionalism provides a climate for discussion, problem-solving, sharing, trust, and persuasion.

By contrast, the dogmatic, closed-minded person makes communication difficult. Such a person says by language, tone, and gesture that he knows it all, and that he is saying everything that is important on the subject. He is combative and argumentative. He is unwilling to submit his opinions and ideas to examination or analysis. He substitutes authority and loudness for evidence and logic. He mistakes his view of the world for reality itself.

THE PROVISIONAL BENEFITS

The benefits of provisionalism to communication are many. We shall look briefly at seven problems that an attitude of provisionalism can help to solve. They are the problems of (1) allness, rigidity, and inflexibility, (2) bypassing, (3) the inference-observation confusion, (4) reflex response, (5) a frozen evaluation about people, (6) a frozen evaluation about things, and (7) escalated conflict.

1. *The Problem of Allness, Rigidity, and Inflexibility*. Allness is an attitude that mistakenly assumes that one can know and be sure of everything about a person, situation, or topic. It also assumes that this knowledge is stationary or permanent, and therefore applicable regardless of time, place, or circumstance.

With many topics, we are like blind scholars each with our hands on a different part of a 14,000-pound pachyderm, but often thinking we are describing the entire elephant. Therefore, we blindly argue our "truth" has a wall (side), spear (tusk), snake (squirming six-foot trunk), tree (leg), fan (ear), or rope (tail). We often forget that descriptive communication is a process of abstracting; that is, we focus on some details while omitting others. The provisional person places a mental "et cetera" after every description.

What is often called "the generation gap" is essentially a communicative allness problem. Donald comes to Dad to share a problem. But before it is heard in full, Donald is interrupted: "When I was a boy . . ." and the definitive and final answer is given. Donald protests that things are different now, all to no avail. Soon Donald stops coming to Dad with his problems. The world is only as Dad sees it—or saw it 20 years ago.

What are the implications for an organization, secular or religious? Despite rapidly shifting conditions, many leaders allow rigid strategies of previously devised plans to keep them from achieving their goals. In today's volatile climate, one cannot run over his problems like a fullback with head down. The executive must run more like a halfback, a broken-field runner, adjusting to obstacles. There is no substitute for continual judgment and reevaluation. Executives of Ford Motor Company have admitted there was evidence that the Edsel automobile was a loser over a year before its introduction in the marketplace. Heavy investment kept them blind to the data of market research.

Lawrence Appley, past president of the American Management Association, writes: "Before the executive can communicate effectively, or in fact handle any of the other tasks of management, he must first know that he doesn't know."[3] When conditions change, our perceptions and strategies must change also or we will be marching to an unsuccessful, anachronistic beat.

What are the implications for the church? We must be careful to distinguish between vital doctrines, which are clearly supported by Scripture, and inconsequential teachings which are open for discussion. In the first category we may place soteriology, the doctrine of salvation. We can say with the Apostle Paul, "I *know* whom I have believed" (2 Timothy 1:12). In the second category we may place the commentary on the "sons of God" recorded in Genesis 6:2. Some, like Finis Dake, teach that these "sons of God" were the fallen angels of 1 Peter 3:19; 2 Peter 2:4; and Jude 6, 7. These angels, it is claimed, married earthly women, producing giants.

---

[3] Lawrence A. Appley, "Is Management Training Worth It?" *Nation's Business* (Nov. 1957), p. 115.

THE ELEMENT OF PROVISIONALISM

Supposedly, it was an attempt by Satan to corrupt the seed through which Christ would come.[4]

This teaching may be true, but this subject certainly is open to other interpretations. We must not confuse the trustworthiness or infallibility of Scripture with commentary or teachings about Scripture. In our language and tone we need an attitude of provisionalism, allowing room for opposing or complementary points of view. No Bible teacher has all the answers. No commentary has the last word.

Further, we must distinguish between sermonizing or application for our spiritual edification and the teaching of Scripture itself. It is one thing to apply details of a parable to our Christian life. It is quite another matter to make a dogmatic doctrine out of these details. Take, for example, the Parable of the Ten Virgins, five wise and five foolish. No doctrine can be based on the oil in their lamps, but applications properly abound. A parable is a story to teach an important lesson disclosed at the end. The lesson here is that we should watch, for we "know neither the day nor the hour" of Christ's return (Matthew 25:1-13).

Another serious problem arises when the Christian leader calls all of his ideas "the leading of the Lord." It is difficult for a church council to give adequate counsel to a minister when vision also includes the only method for achieving that vision. We can be positive about the vision without being inflexible about methods and schedules to implement that vision.

---

[4] Dake's *Annotated Reference Bible*, p. 17.

It is catastrophic when we become morally blind and claim that God is leading some evil or ignoble purpose. A case in point is The Thirty Years' War of Europe (1618-1648) in which rival Christian factions fought each other for political control. The riots of 1844 in Philadelphia, between native-born Protestants and Irish Roman Catholic immigrants resulting in 30 deaths, is another example. Despicable is the long-standing feud between Catholics and Protestants in Ireland today—terrorism and bombs in the name of the Lord! We might also add that God does not support any dishonest methods, however worthy the goal.

The implications for the home are also clear. If both husband and wife are working, it is only fair that both share the household chores. Several guidelines may be given, concerning such an arrangement:

a. Communicate clearly with each other about what needs to be done. It is not possible to do everything.

b. Communicate clearly about what each agrees to do. A time schedule is helpful.

c. Each should do the work he or she finds most enjoyable or least objectionable. Hire outside help if necessary and possible.

d. Set aside time for each other free of pressure. Set aside time for church, pleasure, and friends.

e. Most of all, be flexible. Change your system if the agreement is not working. Experiment with different ways of doing things. Renegotiate before you feel exploited and resentful. Be frank: "Honey, this just isn't working for me." Change allness and rigidity into provisionalism.

THE ELEMENT OF PROVISIONALISM 133

2. *The Problem of Bypassing.* The sending of messages does not insure the understanding of messages. The nonprovisional person assumes that words contain exact meaning. The provisional person realizes that only people have meaning; words are merely symbols of sound, sight, or touch (Braille) waiting for interpretation.

Often the interpretation of the receiver is different from the meaning of the sender. This is true, in part, because the same word can have different definitions. The 500 most commonly used words in our language have an aggregate total of 14,000 dictionary definitions! How many definitions can you think of for the word *fast*? Thus, it is easy for people to hear the same words, but to receive different meanings.

Bypassing sometimes occurs when we use different words, but mean the same thing. Bypassing also occurs when we accent different words. Take the sentence: "I did not say that he stole the money." Now accent the underlined words.

a. **I** did not say that he stole the money.
b. I did **not** say that he stole the money.
c. I did not say that **he** stole the money.
d. I did not say that he **stole** the money.
e. I did not say that he stole the **money**.

Notice the different meanings. A study done for advertisers indicates that television viewers misunderstand from one-fourth to one-third of what they watch, whether it is news, entertainment, or advertising.[5]

---

[5] Jacob Jacoby and a team of Purdue researchers. A May, 1980, study done for the Educational Foundation of the American Association of Advertising Agencies.

One of many things we have learned from cybernetics is the importance of feedback. The provisional person questions and paraphrases to increase accuracy. He is approachable and does not become irritable when asked for clarification. He is person-oriented, not word-oriented, and is sensitive to context both verbally and situationally.

Quite naturally, studies confirm that two-way communication is much more effective than one-way communication. Face-to-face communication is the most effective single medium because it allows for maximum feedback. Face-to-face communication followed by written verification is the most effective overall. It allows for maximum feedback while providing information for later reference. The provisional person checks to determine the effectiveness of his communication. He knows how easy it is to misunderstand.

3. *The Inference-Observation Confusion.* The provisional person distinguishes observation from inference. He is interested in the facts behind the judgment. He labels his inferences and helps others to label theirs. He separates the facts from his opinions about the facts. He is aware that the *is* of identification (this *is* a book) and the *is* of fact (one plus one *is* two) differs from the *is* of evaluation (Marilyn *is* dishonest/or beautiful/or ugly). The last *is* is one of judgment or opinion, not necessarily one of fact.

4. *The Problem of Reflex Response.* The provisional person strives for suspended judgment. He is aware of the dangers of thalamic reaction. When someone says or does something that triggers an emotional response, it is tempting to "fly off the handle," to react without thinking, to make a snap judgment.

The thalamus is a mass of gray matter in the lower part of the brain. It normally channels sensory impressions to the cortex before signaling the muscles for action. The cortex is the outer layer of gray matter covering most of the brain. It distinguishes sensory impressions and correlates them with past knowledge and experience. It weighs various courses of action. In an emergency, the thalamus bypasses the cortex, providing a reflex action such as slamming on the brakes when a child darts in front of the car.

The provisional person allows the cortex time to consider evidence before reacting. He allows the cortex, not the thalamus, to control the emotions. He slows down and thinks before reacting. He suspends judgment until he has sufficient evidence and has weighed that evidence. The Bible says, "He who is slow to anger has great understanding, but he who has a hasty temper exalts folly" (Proverbs 14:29).

Suspended judgment is a key to sound decision-making. Suppose, for example, that you go to hear a well-known speaker. You are surprised at his manner of speech. He slurs his words so noticeably that you conclude that he must have been drinking. His content is presented so pessimistically that you wonder how he could be known for his positive mental attitude. You leave disappointed and dismayed.

Later you learn that shortly after the speech, the speaker had surgery to remove a glioma, the worst kind of cancerous brain tumor. You also learn that when you heard him, he was heavily sedated with prescribed drugs to relieve severe pain. What is your judgment now? Are you happy about what you said to your friends?

Or suppose that you drive into the parking lot of a drugstore. A severe thunderstorm is underway and you don't have an umbrella. All the close parking spaces are taken. One automobile is parked diagonally taking up two spaces right at the drugstore entrance. Your blood pressure rises. You become perceptibly annoyed. On the way into the store you see the young man who has misparked. You utter some uncomplimentary words about his inconsiderate hogging of space. He ignores you and takes off with the sound of screeching tires.

You repeat your remarks about him to the store clerk. The clerk tells you that the young man's mother was hurt seriously in an automobile accident a couple of blocks away. He had rushed to the drugstore to telephone for an ambulance. How do you feel now? Would you like to retract your remarks to the young man?

In dealing with young children, parents must learn early that the stories told them are often highly colored. In business, the executive must become aware that upward communication is highly distorted as the subordinate wishes to look good in the boss's eyes. Then too, sufficient data is not always readily available. The president of a large corporation conducted an executive meeting on a proposed venture. Each person in turn presented glowing remarks supporting the project. Then the president asked for reasons against the proposal. None were forthcoming. "I can't think of any objections either," the president said, "so let's table the discussion until we have done sufficient homework." Three weeks later they met again. With sufficient data, they scrapped the project!

The provisional person distinguishes in his communication between statistics, observations, studies, names, and other specifics, on the one hand, and generalizations, judgments, assumptions, opinions, and inferences, on the other hand. The provisional communicator also suspends judgment. He avoids thalamic reactions allowing his cortex to rule the emotions. He waits for sufficient data before making an important decision. Sometimes it is as simple as saying, "I would like to give your idea more thought," or "Let me sleep on that." How many times have we seen things differently with a little time to consider?

5. A Frozen Evaluation About People. John was a first-quarter freshman in a class I taught one fall some years ago. He was having personal problems. Eventually he had to drop all of his classes that quarter except mine which he struggled through earning the grade of C.

John also had gotten into trouble with the law. He was caught for stealing hubcaps on the university parking lot. We talked together for many hours that quarter. We talked about values, honesty, goals, motivation, direction, even a commitment to God. John made an about-face. So great was his change, that he made all *A*'s in the rest of his college course work. As his adviser through the four years, I watched his growth and development in his person and in his faith.

Quite naturally, I wrote an exuberant recommendation when John applied to a prestigious law school. A couple of weeks later, I received a phone call from the dean of the law school. His opening remarks were, "Apparently you don't know John as well as you think you do. Our investigation has disclosed that John is a thief. We don't accept anyone with a police record."

I replied, "Are you referring to a hubcap incident in his freshman year?"

"Yes," said the dean.

"Well," I said, "John incoming freshman is not John graduating senior. Your hubcaps are safe. I hope you won't make the mistake of the frozen evaluation. People can change, and John's change over the past four years is remarkable."

John was accepted into the law school. He is an outstanding young attorney today!

Provisional parents communicate to their children in such a way as to recognize change, growth, responsibility, and development as they mature into adults. The provisional executive allows for and expects growth in his personnel. The provisional church leader watches for growth also. He is not bound to a frozen evaluation. Growth is recognized and rewarded with trust and responsibility. Mistakes of the past are forgotten.

Paul and Barnabas foolishly destroyed a precious friendship. They split up as missionaries over whether the young John Mark, who had deserted them at Perga during their first missionary journey, should be allowed to accompany them on their second missionary journey. Barnabas felt that his nephew had matured and was worthy of another chance. Paul did not. A decade later, Paul acknowledged that Mark had grown spiritually and requested his companionship (Acts 13:13; 15:36-39; 2 Timothy 4:11; Colossians 4:1). Second-century writers report that Mark, in the meantime, had an extensive ministry with Barnabas and Peter. This same Mark became the author of our second Gospel.

6. *A Frozen Evaluation About Things*. A frozen evaluation about people or things is a judgment set in concrete. A frozen judgment becomes inaccurate, outdated, and unrealistic as people, attitudes, situations, and objects change.

In 1950 Ted Williams, the famous Boston Red Sox baseball slugger, signed a $125,000 contract. Sportswriters at the time called it a "record" salary and labeled Williams "the highest-paid player in baseball history." By comparison, Babe Ruth, perhaps the greatest baseball slugger ever, made only $80,000 playing for the New York Yankees in 1930 and 1931.

The provisional person, however, applies the time index. He does not assume that a dollar in 1950 is the same as a dollar in 1931. Inflation had shrunk the dollar after 1931 so that a 1950 dollar was worth only 57 cents in comparison. The federal tax structure had changed so that Williams took home $62,028 after taxes while Ruth took home $68,535. For Ted Williams to have had as much buying power with his take-home pay as Babe Ruth, he would have had to make $327,451!

In 1972 Henry Aaron, who had more home runs than any man in history, made $200,000 playing for the Atlanta Braves. Aaron would have needed to make over $600,000 to equal the salary of Babe Ruth!

In the five years between 1975 and 1980, the average worker's after-tax income rose 69 percent. At first glance, it looks like the average worker had unparalleled good fortune and prosperity. Actually, the same average worker suffered a 4-percent loss in buying power after his earnings were adjusted for inflation. This means that if a church had paid its pastor $20,000 in 1975, it would have had to pay him $34,600 to equal that amount in 1980.

The provisional person does not fight change and progress. When street lights first appeared in New York City, some ministers cried out against them because the Bible says, "God made the two great lights, the greater light to rule the day, and the lesser light to rule the night" (Genesis 1:16). How could the moon rule the night, they reasoned, if there were street lights?

When the steam locomotive made its initial run, some churches were quick to condemn "the monster that belched smoke like that of hell." When the radio was invented, some sincere Christians called it a "witch's box." For years after its debut, television was condemned from the pulpit. True, there are unacceptable programs on television and the Christian must practice selectivity. Yet the church cannot ignore a medium that reaches the average home over six hours a day! Congratulations to the ministers who have used this medium for God!

When the United States was first preparing to send a satellite into orbit, sincere Christians warned of calamity. After all, did not God confound man's language when he attempted to build the Tower of Babel? Archaeologists have found the ruins of the tower. If it had been completed, it would not have exceeded 300 feet! Modern skyscrapers are four times that high. Thank God for leaders like Pat Robertson who saw the potential of the communication satellites for the gospel message!

Do not think for a moment that only the church has the problem of accepting change. When the bathtub was invented around 1840, it was condemned as a dangerous health hazard! And by whom was it condemned? The Boston Medical Society—a group of physicians—cried out against it! A provisional attitude prepares us for change.

Provisionalism helps us to break out of our preconceived limitations. Try your hand at an interesting problem: Draw nine dots as follows:

```
•   •   •

•   •   •

•   •   •
```

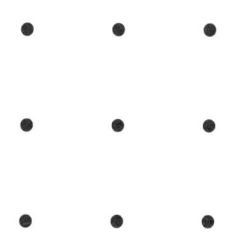

Start with your pencil on any dot. Draw four straight lines joining all the dots without removing your pencil. You may cross lines, but you may not retrace any. Try the puzzle before checking the solution on the next page.

Here is another problem. Write the Roman numeral IX. Now, by writing just one symbol, change the Roman numeral to the number 6. Try the experiment before checking the answer on the next page.

Now check the solutions. You became successful the moment you became provisional and broke out of the crippling limitation of the imaginary square or the confinement to Roman numerals. In a similar manner many problems require a new definition to achieve solution.

7. *The Problem of Escalating Conflict.* Perhaps the most familiar and disruptive problem of all communication occurs when calm discussion degenerates into heated argument. Emotion supplants reason. Talk escalates into vituperation—shouting, blaming, name-calling, threat, and ultimatum. On the playground, conflict can boil into a fist fight. In the home, it can clamor toward the divorce court or alienate parent and child. On the job, it can precipitate a firing or dissolve a partnership. On the national scene, 1,787 murders in

New York City and 1,040 in Los Angeles last year—over 22,000 nationwide—tell us that vidlence is epidemic in America. Family fights that zoomed out of control were high on the list of reasons for homicide. On the international scene, we are reminded of the seemingly endless lines of plain stones that furrow The Fields of the Dead at Arlington National Cemetery.

The problem of escalated conflict can be corrected when we understand the psychology of the pendulum effect. Whenever we speak, we presume our perception of reality is accurate, on dead center, as illustrated by the pendulum in the middle position.

Solution (1) (page 141) | Solution (2) (page 141)

IX Changed to 6:

SIX

Whenever we hear someone else respond, we perceive him to be off-center if he does not agree with us. This may be illustrated by the pendulum to the right of center.

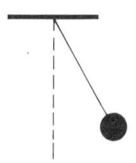

When we hear what we perceive to be off-center, we tend to balance the discussion by remarks equally to the left of center—a position more extreme and dogmatic than the one we really hold.

This more extreme position by us causes our listener the psychological problem of balancing what we just said. Hence he goes even further to the right in his comments.

The vicious swing often continues until both are shouting and saying things we don't really mean.

The provisional person recognizes that what is dead center to him might be off-center to someone else. He, therefore, seeks to close the gap rather than psychologically balance and widen the gap. He seeks common ground while speaking softly. He restates the position of the other to show understanding and insight into the person's world of thought and emotions. He shares where he is coming from without trying to hammer his ideas down the throat of the other. He invites a search for a solution mutually acceptable when compromise is necessary. If they must differ, the channels for constructive dialogue are kept open for future exploration. Hence, conflict is diffused rather than escalated.

Conflict is also escalated by polarized or disjunctive thinking; that is, we tend to see things in terms of just two sides, two opposite positions, tendencies, or principles. Our language is faulty in part. We have many antonyms such as *good* and *evil*, *success* and *failure*, *polite* and *rude*, *sweet* and *sour*, *right* and *wrong*, *black* and *white*. But we have few words to express middle ground. Try to give a neutral middle term halfway between the antonyms above and note the difficulty.

The provisional person diffuses conflict by recognizing that issues are many-sided rather than two-sided. He also recognizes that many positions are neither right nor wrong, just different. Plans A and B may be good and better, rather than right or wrong. Plan C, which would combine the best features of A and B or eliminate some negative aspects of each, may emerge after discussion. Conflict is healthy and inevitable in viable relationships, both business and personal. Escalated conflict is unhealthy and divisive, and falls far short of the spirit of Christ.

THE PROVISIONAL PROFILE

We all know some provisional persons. They constantly search beyond the boundaries of their present knowledge.

They refuse to be chained by yesterday or even by today.

They are teachable, malleable, approachable. They never stop learning, searching, or listening. They are viable seeds, a constant source of growth.

They embrace today's wisdom and knowledge but add a new dimension or perspective to it.

They have a solid faith no one can shake. Yet they know the difference between belief and bigotry. They know the difference between knowledge and dogmatism.

They keep aware of the limits of their own knowledge. They know that they do not know it all on any topic. They seek, inquire, wonder, and query rather than argue, rebut, dismiss, and deny.

We also all know unprovisional people. They are stunted, dwarfed, dead while living. Regardless of their age, they are old fogies.

They refuse to grow, to move, to develop. They are contented to stay where they are, spiritually and mentally. The best is always the past.

They embrace only the old and familiar. They have frozen their thinking. They have narrowed their wavelengths. They are stuck in yesterday or "the good old days." They are negative to anything new or different.

They are imprisoned in the little dusty dungeons of their own impoverished minds.

They are the complainers, the grumblers, and the instigators of conflict.

God's people strive to be provisional in all their relationships with others.

SUMMARY

Provisionalism is an attitude of open-mindedness, flexibility, and adaptability. The provisional person constantly seeks deeper understanding, sharper definition, greater accuracy, and expanded truth. He believes that better methods are waiting to be discovered and new knowledge waiting to be perceived. He sees himself and his ideas open to change, development, and growth. Provisionalism is supported solidly by Scripture, history, and psychology.

An attitude of provisionalism benefits communication in at least seven ways:

1. It helps us overcome the problem of thinking we know it all, however great our education, training, or experience. It opens us to other people, ideas, and methods.

2. Provisionalism helps us overcome the problem of bypassing by alerting us to the fact that the sending of messages does not insure the understanding of messages. Words do not contain meaning. Rather, they are symbols that evoke meanings in us, which may or may not resemble that of the sender. Feedback, listening, questioning, and paraphrasing are programmed into crucial communication.

3. Provisionalism forces us to separate inference from observation in our communication, and to separate the *is* of identification and the *is* of fact from the *is* of evaluation. It also forces us to question observation, even our own, and to improve our observational techniques. People in general are poor observers. Memory is frequently an unconscious mixture of fact and fiction, observation and judgment, with adults as well as children. Those who forget history, Santayana reminds us, are condemned to repeat it. To that we might add: Those who remember history are condemned to revise it.

4. Provisionalism helps us to communicate more effectively by reminding us to avoid a verbal reflex response to the speech and action of others. It enables the cortex to override the thalamus. Suspended judgment, until all the evidence is weighed, improves the tone of communication and the quality of decision-making.

5. Provisionalism avoids the frozen evaluation of people. People can mature, develop, and grow. Communication is directed toward present performance and away from class stereotyping or character assassination. The provisional executive or church leader allows for mistakes and promotes growth in his personnel or membership. Communication is charitable, descriptive, motivational, inspirational, and encouraging rather than judgmental.

6. The provisional person avoids a frozen evaluation about things and circumstances. He does not fight change, innovation, or progress. Change, whether progress or retreat, is inevitable. Even to hold one's own

requires dynamic action and adjustment of sails against the winds of change. The communication of the provisional person is relevant rather than reactionary, positive rather than negative, dynamic rather than static, and contemporary rather than anachronistic.

7. Provisionalism helps us avoid the communicative problem of escalated conflict. The provisional person emphasizes common ground rather than differences. Like the wise parent dealing with a confused high school senior, he leaves the door of dialogue open for the future when experience might teach the truth of previous counsel. Perspectives are shared without demanding conformity. Issues are not forced into two sides, one right and the other wrong. Rather, issues are recognized as many-sided with advantages and disadvantages associated with each position. The Christian strives for provisionalism with other Christians and with non-Christians as well. Christ, as the answer to life's problems, can only be shared—not forced. When the Apostle Paul described himself as the foremost of sinners in the introduction to his first letter to Timothy, we can be sure his communication was better received by the young man than if he had set himself up as some paragon of virtue (1 Timothy 1:15).

5

EMPATHIC UNDERSTANDING

Another ingredient of a communicative climate is empathic understanding whereby we intellectually and emotionally identify with others. This ingredient enables us to come into another's world of experience, to stand in his shoes, to feel his hurt, and to share his joy.

Each of us lives in a different psychological environment, which we call "our perceptual world." Our perceptual world may be likened to a room with one opening, greatly limiting our vision of the vast world outside. Worse yet, we cannot see through this one window directly with undistorted perception. As the Apostle Paul expressed it to the Church at Corinth, we only see the outside as reflected through a clouded mirror (1 Corinthians 13:12).

My perceptual world differs from yours even if we come from the same part of the country, the same city, the same suburb, or even the same home. Hence, the world of the first child can be a million psychological miles from the world of the second child. The world of the parent is not the world of the child. Likewise, the world of the boss is not the world of the subordinate. In a sampling of top management, nine out of ten were positive that subordinates felt "very free" to discuss important aspects of the job with them. When those same subordinates were interviewed, however, only six out of every ten agreed.[1] At one point the worlds of Peter and Paul were divided sharply over the question: Should Gentiles be required to practice the Jewish ritual of circumcision (Galatians 2)?

DIFFERENT STIMULI

In many ways our perceptual world may be likened to a radio. Despite the myriad of waves on varying frequency lengths, we can tune in on only one station at a time. Perceptually, we tune in one set of stimuli while selectively ignoring an infinite number of other sets.

By and large, our station selection is based on needs. As needs change, so does perception. Needs constantly keep ahead of selection. Needs of the moment prepare us for the perception of the next moment. The more relevance something has for our needs, the greater chance that it will catch our perceptual attention. It has been my experience that it takes the average minister out of seminary about three years to learn that

---

[1] Rensis Likert, *New Patterns of Management* (New York: McGraw-Hill Book Co., Inc., 1961), p. 47.

an ounce of illustration and application is worth a pound of theory and exegesis.

Learning follows a pattern similar to perception. Learning may be described as coming into a new world by bridging the known and the unknown. By and large, the instruction remembered consists of those things that reinforce prior concepts. The more landmarks or signposts, variations, and distinctions a teacher can place on a student's road of learning, the more he can learn. Or put another way, the more hooks a teacher can place in the student's closet of learning, the more places he can hang his hat of reference. It is almost impossible to take the second year of chemistry before taking the first year. Without giving some preparation in prophecy, the minister may find that his congregation is not agog over Gog and Magog recorded in the books of Ezekiel and Revelation (Revelation 20:8; Ezekiel 38: 2, 9, 15).

If your audience or class seems dull and you think you may be casting your pearls before swine, consider first the pearls. As communicators, it is our responsibility to come into the other person's world of perceptual experience: to speak through his needs, his worries, his concerns; to speak through those things close to his previous learning. Otherwise, we lose him. He cannot tune us in even if he so desires. That which is unfamiliar or seemingly irrelevant becomes static and noise, causing perceptual distortion and inattentiveness.

One quarter while I was teaching a class on the psychology of advertising, a girl handed in an assignment suggesting the following slogan for a bank: "Jesus saves. Why don't you?" Upon chatting with her, I found she was not facetious. Coming from a totally irreligious home, she had no concept of salvation. To a new generation of the unchurched, we have an unprecedented challenge and responsibility to relate to their perceptual world. Rather than condemning others for not responding to our channel, we must take the responsibility to get on their frequency. This is achieved, in part, by identifying with their needs, motives, language, longings, feelings, joys, fears, and frustrations.

It is also achieved by immersion into another's culture. This is incredibly important when communicating to nationals of another country or when communicating to subcultures within our own country. General Motors could not sell its Chevrolet Nova in South America because *No va* in Spanish means "It won't go"!

DIFFERENT SENSORY RECEPTORS

We can witness more effectively and understand others better if we remember that no two people have identical sensory receptors. To illustrate this point to my class, the psychology of communication, I bring in a sheet of paper coated with the chemical phenylthiocarbamide, commonly called PTC. If the class is representative of the general population, approximately half will experience nothing at all when they touch their tongue to a piece of paper. They will think that I am putting them on. Most of the remaining half will taste the paper as bitter, but some will find it sweet, others will find it sour, and still others will call it salty!

About 6 percent of our adult male population (and about 0.5 percent of our female population) has some kind of color blindness. Most problems concern the color red; some, the color green; and a very few persons see no color at all. My college roommate in my freshman year had the last difficulty. All life for him was seen on a black and white TV set. I would like to tell you that I was a kind, considerate roommate. I must confess, however, that I was occasionally frolicsome, sending him on a date in the most outlandish color combinations.

A few people can see a fraction of the ultraviolet range. This makes their red significantly different from the red of most. Even if we fall within the general population, our reds differ. As we learned in physics, electromagnetic or light waves have no color. Color is our perceptual and personal optic response to the reflection of light.

Our thresholds of pain differ widely, both physically and psychologically. My younger son, like his mother, approaches the dentist's chair calmly, disdaining any anesthetic. The numbness is a greater irritant than the drill. Even our dentist is amazed at his immunity to pain. My older son, like me, twitches, shakes, and quakes at the thought of a drill. Bring on the needle—by far the lesser of two evils!

The average person hears in a range of 125 to 12,000 hz (cycles per second). Yet some hear as low as 25; others, as high as 20,000. If your wife insists that she hears a squeal in the TV, don't call her crazy simply because you can't hear it. She may be sensitive in a range where you are deaf. The noise pollution of our generation is reducing our capacity to hear!

It's easy, of course, to realize that "beauty is in the eye of the beholder." Few of us get upset over another's taste in food. Nor do we mind another's taste in music so long as we don't have to listen to it. Likewise, we easily understand color blindness, differing thresholds of pain, and differing ranges of hearing. We tend to forget, however, that a person's entire perceptual world is resident in the mind. Much that we disagree about is not the event itself, but rather our perception of that event. Whether or not 10-year-old Jack is bad or merely mischievous depends on our perception of Jack's behavior. It boils down to an argument over us and our perceptual worlds, not over Jack at all. Calling someone "crazy" because of his perception makes about as much sense as denying someone's taste or pain. We must come into his world to communicate.

The Gospel of John records an interesting perceptual phenomenon that took place on Palm Sunday. While the crowd bustled around Him, awed over the recent resurrection of Lazarus, Jesus thought of the impending cross and unburdened Himself in prayer. Jesus closed with the request: "Father, glorify thy name." Then a voice came from heaven saying, "I have glorified it, and I will glorify it again." The crowd standing by heard it. Some thought it "thundered," but others said, "An angel has spoken to him" (John 12:13, 17, 27-29).

People differ in their sensory perception physically, psychologically, and spiritually. We all have our areas of imperception. We have eyes, but we see not. We have ears, but hear only thunder. Empathic communication attempts to reach the other's wavelength.

DIFFERENT PSYCHOLOGICAL SETS

"I'll be seeing you in all the old familiar places, that this heart of mine embraces" is more than sentimental pining by a lonely or rejected suitor. It is psychological reality. After a romantic breakup, it is not uncommon for one to fight the tears upon returning alone to a favorite restaurant or upon hearing a song that once had special meaning for two.

This is our psychological set at work. Events in our past experience cause us to react to more than the sensory perception before us. We react to associations, overtones, and feelings. We make signal responses along habitual patterns. Take the person who has not learned to handle teasing, for example. Each new episode conjures up unpleasant associations of past embarrassment. A sharp tongue may be a defensive signal of habitual response.

Observe Bill, the salesman, at the end of a rough week. Sales are down, commissions are down, and Bill is down. The sales manager has applied his pressure first by a pep talk, second by listing Bill last on the weekly sales chart, and last by chewing him out. Now Bill comes home. Before he can get his coat off, his wife Sue greets him with Scott's need of a baseball glove for Little League and Amy's need for a new pair of shoes. Bill explodes while Sue throws up her hand in amazement: "What did I do? What did I say?"

The timing was poor. Things look different after a warm greeting, a good meal, and the sports page. But Bill, too, has a problem. He responds in an ugly manner to pressure. Under pressure almost anything can trigger his habitual response. The boss takes his frustrations out on Bill. Bill screams at his wife. The wife boils over on the kids. And the kids mistreat the cat as the ripples of frustration widen.

To a large extent our psychological set resembles a motion picture. The events of one frame prepare or condition us for the next. A risky operation is being performed. The skilled surgeon labors to save her life. The nervous husband paces in the waiting room. A glance at the flourescent screen of the oscilloscope reveals that vital signs are weakening. And we are caught up in the drama—all by a film editor's design.

The wise communicator is aware of the importance of psychological sets. Timing is important. Atmosphere is important. Studies show that people are more persuadable after a good dinner. Important also are language, gesture, tone, and attitude. Getting along with others is a skill that can be developed. So is persuasion. Much of the time what we see while communicating with others is really their reaction to us, not to our proposal. Perhaps I have evaluated you, questioned your motives, disapproved of your actions. Perhaps I have attempted to control you, to change your attitude or behavior. Perhaps I have tried to manipulate you. Maybe I have acted superior with you, giving the impression that I know it all. If so, chances are you will become defensive and react in some customary manner, which usually includes rejection.

Just one ill-chosen word may be the culprit. A Black, for example, may not hear another word after being called *boy* by a White. The word *colored* was offensive, *Negro* acceptable, *Black* preferred by Blacks in a 1973 study. In 1968 the word *Black* was offensive, *Afro-American* liked, and *Negro* preferred.[2] Recently in St. Louis a white man was attacked by a Black when "complimented" for being "a good Samaritan." He thought the term was derogatory.

Words trigger psychological sets. Which would you rather eat—*chateaubriand* or *dead cow*? Job long ago

---

[2] "Negro, Colored or Black?" *The Detroit News* (September 8, 1968), p. 1. "Black Is Beautiful to Most Blacks," *The Detroit News* (June 13, 1973), p. 25.

spoke of some words that "break [us] in pieces" and others that make us stand (Job 19:2; 6:25). We live in a world of words. Words are the most important tools at our command. Some words inflame, deflate, and discourage; others soothe, inspire, and invigorate.

It was eight years to the day from the Battles of Lexington and Concord (April 19, 1775) to the victory of Washington over Cornwallis at Yorktown (1781) and the final armistice (April 19, 1783). What an insurmountable task General Washington faced! Soldiers generally enlisted for short periods. When they felt like going home to harvest crops or to see their families or for any other reason, they just deserted. Soldiers were reluctant to fight far from their homes. There was little regimentation, discipline, or authority. Pay was poor, and sometimes nonexistent. Often there were insufficient uniforms, coats, and blankets to go around. From a large number of summer soldiers and sunshine patriots, Washington's army dwindled from 22,000 to 2,400 in the winter of 1776. Washington had lost the Battles of Long Island, Brooklyn, and Manhattan and had retreated to Pennsylvania. "The game is pretty near up," George wrote his brother. "However, under a full persuasion of the justice of our cause, I cannot entertain an idea that it will finally sink, though it may remain for some time under a cloud."[3] Yet in the sleet and snow of Christmas night, overcoming his own doubts, Washington inspired his meager army to cross the ice-choked Delaware River and surprise the powerful Hessian army of mercenaries at Trenton.

---

[3] George Washington, *Writings*, ed. John C. Fitzpatrick, 30 vol. (1931-1944). Letter to his brother Augustine (December, 1776).

Washington was no military genius. He made many tactical errors and sometimes grave blunders. His genius lay in his ability with words. He could inspire faith and diffuse his own courage among his soldiers. He could rally small battalions to fight large regiments, pressing for ultimate victory despite temporary losses and heartbreaking setbacks. His words could trigger psychological sets of patriotism and courage. The Battle of Trenton that Yuletide night is credited with saving the American Revolution!

More than anything else, we must guard against words that threaten another person's ego. Nothing will trigger a reaction faster. Never make a person feel like a fool any time. Never make a person lose face—especially in the presence of others. When we disturb a person's dignity, we disturb *him*. A psychological set is aroused, and he naturally seeks to protect himself at all costs. If in our faulty communication we attack someone's self-respect, we invite trouble to our organization. As a witness, we hurt the cause of Christ.

DIFFERENT FRAMES OF REFERENCE

A display advertisement in a grocery store is designed to appeal to impulse-buying. It seeks to evoke a psychological set by appealing to the immediate senses or by reminding us of some recent television commercial. Our frame of reference, on the other hand, is our standards and values—our attitudes and beliefs developed over a long period of time.

Our frame of reference is our internal reality and the only door we have to the appraisal of external reality. Our frame of reference drastically changes when we become a Christian. The Bible says, "The unspiritual man does not receive the gifts of the Spirit of God, for they are folly to him, and he is not able to understand them because they are spiritually discerned" (1 Corinthians 2:14). To the unregenerated man, "the preaching of the cross is foolishness"; to the Christian, "it is the power of God" (1 Corinthians 1:18).

Being Christians, however, does not obliterate different frames of reference even within the camp of Evangelicals. When I attended seminary at Wheaton Graduate School of Theology, three views were taught concerning 1 Corinthians 15:51—"Lo! I tell you a mystery. We shall not all sleep, but we shall all be changed, in a moment, in the twinkling of an eye, at the last trumpet. For the trumpet will sound, and the dead will be raised imperishable, and we shall be changed."

Dr. Kenneth Kantzer, who later became dean of Trinity Seminary and editor in chief of *Christianity Today*, taught that this verse refers to a Rapture in which all believers past and present will suddenly rise and be with Christ. This event will occur before the Great Tribulation, a seven-year period of misery such as the world has never known, and therefore at least seven years before the second coming of Christ. This is the position of most Evangelical Christians.

Dr. Merrill C. Tenney, then dean of the school, also taught a Rapture. His took place in the middle of the Great Tribulation, three and one-half years before the second coming of Christ. Pat Robertson embraces this position and is trying to prepare Christians to survive during the Tribulation.

Dr. Beckerly Michelson, who later went to Bethany Seminary, taught that the concept of a Rapture was unbiblical. He claimed that the doctrine dated no earlier then the 1800s. His position is that there is only one event, the second coming of Christ, which will take place after the Great Tribulation.

It was not a matter of knowledge with my Wheaton professors. Each was keenly aware of the other positions and the evidence used to support those positions. When discussing the topic, each launched his doctrinal boat into the same sea of data from the same port of scriptural authority. Each raised his sails into the same winds of reasoning, logic, analysis, and original language exegesis. The set of the sails differed, however, causing each to arrive at dissenting destinations.

And what about us students, each a budding Apollo, listening eagerly to every word proceeding out of the mouths of our professors? We all came to graduate school with at least two years of Greek and took more while there. By the time we were ready to make our mark on the world, we could gargle in Greek, dream in Hebrew, and have visions in Aramaic. The best reference works were set at our fingertips. What about us? By and large we tended to rally behind the professor who voiced our frame of reference developed over the years from our parents, pastors, and churches.

This reaction is typical. Studies firmly indicate that early definitions usually take precedence over later definitions, determining our interpretations of subsequent data. Unaware of our serious problem, we distort new messages to conform to previous learning and communicative patterns. The more emotionally involved we are with the topic or decision, the more we selectively, yet unconsciously, distort data inputs that disturb our preconceived images or opinions.[4] It is important for us to be charitable with other Christians whose frames of reference differ from ours.

Historical accounts covering the same events highlight the problem of different frames of reference. How shall we describe the war of 1861-1865 between the North and the South? Union writers and statesmen of the time called it a Civil War, which means a war between geographical sections or political factions of the same nation. As early as January of 1830, Daniel Webster voiced the position of the North: "Liberty and union, now and forever, on and inseparable."[5]

In that tradition, Abraham Lincoln came to office March 4, 1861. South Carolina, Mississippi, Florida, Alabama, and Georgia legislatures had already voted to secede from the Union. Others would soon follow. Upon resigning from the United States Senate, Jefferson Davis of Mississippi spoke for all of the departing states begging to leave in peace: "You may make war on a foreign state. If it be the purpose of gentlemen, they may make war against a state which has withdrawn from the Union; but there are no laws of the United States to be executed within the limits of a seceded state."[6]

Some historians argue that there would have been

---

[4] See, for example, the studies of Hans Sebald, "Limitations of Communication: Mechanisms of Image Maintenance in Form of Selective Perception, Selective Memory, and Selective Distortion," *Journal of Communication*, Vol. XII, No. 3 (September, 1962), and D. T. Cambell, "Systematic Error on the Part of Human Links in Communication Systems," *Information and Control*, Vol. I (1958).

[5] Daniel Webster's speech before the Senate, January 26, 27, 1830.

[6] On December 29, 1860, South Carolina seceded, followed by the other southern states in a matter of weeks. Jefferson Davis gave his farewell address to the Senate on January 21, 1861. He was elected president of the Confederacy, February 9.

no war if Stephen Douglas had been elected President instead of Lincoln. The states would have been allowed to secede. To the South it was not a Civil War, but a War Between the States. Under the Articles of Confederation, and from Independence Day, 1776, to 1789, the states were separate sovereign powers allied as in a league of nations or confederacy. Then under the Constitution, the states voluntarily granted supreme power to the Union because it seemed best for their welfare, despite the opposition of men like Patrick Henry, the revolutionary star. Against the power of the Crown ("Give me liberty or give me death"), Henry also feared the powers of the President under the proposed Constitution, then without the Bill of Rights.

Divided over such issues as tariffs and slavery, the Confederacy believed that they could secede from the Union just as they had joined. Lincoln made his position clear in his first inaugural address. The seceded states must submit to the Union: "In your hands, my dissatisfied fellow countrymen, and not in mine, is the momentous issue of the Civil War."[7]

Tragically, 360,222 Union and 258,000 Confederacy graves decided the issue—more than our casualties in all other wars combined! The price of different frames of reference was more than 0.5 million lives! Another 0.5 million were wounded!

A PROBLEM OF INFORMATION

Sometimes the problem of different frames of reference is simply one of knowledge. Was George Washington the first President of the United States? Although

---

[7] Lincoln took office March 4, 1861, and gave his first inaugural address.

some elementary school books still perpetuate the myth, we know that Washington never chopped down a cherry tree nor ever threw a silver dollar across the Potomac. (I don't know why our legend ever made a big thing over throwing a dollar across a river. Subsequent Presidents have thrown billions across the Atlantic Ocean, and we have scarcely said a word!)

But was Washington the first President? Some would say no, pointing out that we had 16 Presidents before Washington, Peyton Randolph of Virginia being the first. Some say John Hancock of Massachusetts was the first, since the bold signer of the Declaration of Independence was the President on July 4, 1776, when we declared our separation from the Crown. Others say that John Hanson of Maryland was the first, for while others were called "President of the Continental Congress," Hanson was titled "President of the United States in Congress Assembled." Furthermore, Hanson was President when the last state ratified the Articles of Confederation in 1781, making us an official nation. Perhaps all would agree that Washington was the first President under the Constitution. While the ones before him were heads of government, Washington was our first head of state. In such a discussion, increased knowledge may reconcile different frames of reference.

A PROBLEM OF VESTED INTEREST

If it were just a problem of information, understanding another person and relating to his frame of reference would be relatively easy. More often, we face a problem of vested interest. The person has something vital and personal to gain from a particular perspective. We tend to think and act in what we believe to be our best interest. Therefore, we expect our President-elect to divest himself of any financial holdings that may constitute a conflict between personal aggrandizement and the national welfare. John F. Kennedy, you will recall, placed his tremendous investments in a blind trust.

Both Northern and Southern statesmen in 1861 would have agreed on salient facts of common history. Both sides knew that the individual states were sovereign under the Articles of Confederation, and that little power resided in the Federal government until 1789. The problem was one of special interests. Could the seven states of the deep South, which originally formed the Southern Confederacy, secede from the Union? The question is relatively unimportant. The fact is the seven states found themselves in what they perceived to be an intolerable economic marriage. They wanted a divorce. They wanted out. They left.

They seceded whether they could or not. On February 4, 1861, they formed a Confederacy. They named a capital: Montgomery, Alabama; later Richmond, Virginia. They elected a President, Jefferson Davis, and a Vice-President, Alexander Stephens. They set up their own bureaus and offices, issued their own stamps and money, raised their taxes while flying their own flag, the Stars and Bars. With the firing on Fort Sumter, April 12, 1861, the seven were joined by four states of the upper South. Now they were 11.

We can see that the issue was not primarily one of information. It was essentially a problem of vested interest. Different ideals, different traditions, different aspirations, a depressed economy, and nearly 4 million slaves separated the North and the South. Religious bonds between the two sections snapped. Baptists and Methodists divided into Northern and Southern churches over slavery. Groups that did not divide, like the Presbyterians, were nonetheless torn by dissension.

Whenever a problem of vested interest exists, argumentation and debate are usually futile. The problem itself must be addressed. In my organizational behavior and communication courses, I stress the importance of dealing with dissension quickly and solving the problems of vested interest to the mutual satisfaction of dissenting factions. Smoldering hostilities must be brought out in the open and extinguished. If not, the embers often flare into costly conflagration. What could have been ended with a hand-held fire extinguisher, now needs the men, trucks, and hoses of five fire stations! Problems such as morale, rumor, and grievances must be dealt with promptly.

What about the Civil War? Could it have been avoided without disunion? Probably earlier. But not by the time Lincoln became President. As early as the late 1820s, coals of nullification and secession were ignited. When South Carolina denounced the tariffs of 1828 and 1832 and forbade Federal customs officials from operating in the state, President Andrew Jackson acted immediately with force, warning South Carolina not to obstruct Federal officers. But it was Henry Clay's proposal of a gradual reduction in tariffs that healed the schism.

We had over one-third of a century from the time of obvious trouble to avert the Civil War. England dealt with the issue of slavery and abolished it in the West Indies in 1834. We had far more to keep us together than that which separated us. For example, by the 1850s we had the best railroad system in the world, providing a vast national market for the products of both American farms and factories. But the succession of Presidents—Taylor, Fillmore, Pierce, and Buchanan—

were the weakest since the nation's founding. Drifting from crisis to crisis, and displaying no effective leadership, they ignored the problems that were dividing our country. From 1830 to 1860 it was a race between integration and disintegration. Leaders saw the two paths that stretched before our country, but there were too few with clear eyes and cool heads. Rage preempted reason. Blurred vision concealed compromise. The nation awkwardly stumbled into the abyss of unnecessary war.

Churches and religious organizations are not immune to special-interest groups any more than a nation. Strong leadership is necessary to unite opposing factions. For factions to unite, the needs of both must be met. Problems must be faced squarely, openly, calmly, and speedily in the spirit of Christ. Is is not easier to bridge a crevice than a chasm? When groups polarize or crystallize their thinking, all the logic, information, and communicative skill in the world may not save disunion—to the hurt of the body of Christ.

An untreated problem usually takes the characteristics of an iceberg with 95 percent of the hostility beneath the surface. The Apostle Paul counseled the church at Ephesus: "Do not let the sun go down on your anger" (Ephesians 4:26). Jesus saw early reconciliation with another church member so important that He suggested delaying one's gift to God until the problem can be settled (Matthew 5:23, 24). Whether in a business, church, or home, procrastination only adds the weight of resentment, bitterness, and distrust.

A PROBLEM OF COGNITIVE CONSISTENCY

When we are presented with new information that appears contradictory or inconsistent with our previous learning, and especially with our beliefs, we tend to experience psychological confusion and tension. For the university student it often means a loss of faith and disorientation. Our cognitive systems seek a harmony and balance between the external world as we believe it to be and our latest perception of it. The existence of this tension of dissonance motivates us to seek the relief of consonance.

We are all familiar with biological homeostasis where the body unceasingly and automatically regulates itself to maintain internal balance. For example, the hotter we become, the more diligently our body works to cool us. Dilation of the superficial blood vessels, increased blood circulation in the skin, perspiring with salt which hastens evaporation, and vaporization of water from the lungs are some of the ways the body reduces heat to restore temperature balance.

The motivation toward cognitive balance can be understood as psychological homeostasis. When we are tense because of conflicting new information, we seek perceptual balance. Sometimes we change our view and modify our behavior. But learning that involves a change in self-organization and self-perception is psychologically threatening. Therefore, we tend to resist the option of change. Our mind, seeking consistency, then rejects the data, distorts the data, or reinterprets the data to fit our previous frame of reference. Sometimes we avoid situations and information that would probably increase the dissonance. We tune it out trying not to think about the inconsistency.

Whenever we receive information that we think threatens the foundation of our faith, the dissonance can be particularly traumatic. Some years ago I made a study of students from religious homes who were now graduating from a large state university. A home was considered religious if the student and at least one parent or guardian attended church on a weekly basis. Surprisingly, one-third of Roman Catholics, one-half of Protestants in general, and three-fourths of Evangelicals felt compelled to abandon their faith! Many described their disorientation to the questionnaire in terms of cosmic aloneness and personal emptiness. Some said they avoided all contact with the church now just to avoid a repetitive emotional crisis.

Such experiences are common. Dr. Kenneth Kantzer shared with me three crisis experiences and the men and books that were helpful to see him through while working on his Ph.D. My father had a crisis of faith while attending Albright College. Now retired from an illustrious ministry, he still vividly recalls the disruptive impact of his professors' lectures and the man who helped him put the pieces together again. The key, of course, is to provide a framework to go along with the new data—a framework that can accommodate and organize the new material into a deeper and indomitable faith. Whenever there is threat to a person's perceptual world, the communicator must first deal with the threat.

A PROBLEM OF OBSERVATIONAL AND MEASUREMENT LIMITATIONS

Sometimes the communicator faces the problem of limitation inherent in observation and measurement. This is especially true when we consider matters of faith, theology, epistemology, and philosophy of religion. But there are limits of knowledge, observation, and measurement in all disciplines.

The clinical thermometer was not invented until the time of the Civil War. Before that time we had no precise way of measuring body temperature. We still resort to ancient but unreliable methods of observation when we place a hand on the forehead of a fevered child. If our hand is cold, the head feels warmer. If our hand is hot, the head feels cooler.

Similarly, before Isaac Newton developed the spectrum to analyze light, we did not know that the beautiful colors of the rainbow were caused by the refraction of sunlight in raindrops. Before the instruments of spectroscopy we could not make a chemical analysis of distant stars and galaxies. It was only a short time ago, relatively, that we had no X-ray machines, radar equipment, electron microscopes, infrared photography, oscilloscopes, and a myriad of other observational and measurement devices. These instruments have widened our perceptual world. Our instruments now range from the simple meter or yardstick to the complex instrument systems that launch and control a space vehicle.

Even with instruments, however, there is a problem of measurement. Is it twice as cold at 10 degrees as it is as 20? Hardly.

The desk where I am writing is approximately 30 inches high. I measured it with a yardstick. If I had a set of giant calipers, perhaps I could determine that my desk is 30.025 inches high. This leads to the delusion that if I had a more accurate measuring device, I might be able to determine the exact height of my desk. But such is not the case. If I could reach the atomic level of my desk, I would find an undulating mass of protons and electrons. The problem would be akin to measuring the ocean near the shore. With each ebb and flow of a wave the level would change!

When workers were completing the monumental Gateway Arch in St. Louis, fire hoses had to be used to cool the massive structure. The metal had expanded in the heat, and the final block of the arch would not fit into place.

The Book of Judges records that God instructed Gideon to reduce his army by proclaiming, "Whoever is fearful and trembling, let him return home" (Judges 7:3). The result: 22,000 failed the test of bravery and went back to their families. The 10,000 remaining were still too numerous, so a further test was ordered. Those who drank from the river by kneeling were sent home; 300 men who lapped water putting their hands to their mouths were retained. They had passed a second test, providing an early example of what today is called the successive-hurdles method of personnel selection. Despite all our modern psychological tests, however, we have no exact method of human measurement. We have no way, for example, to measure exact degrees of psychological stress. All zero points on ordinal scales are arbitrarily assigned. When a person does not know where he started from, he cannot determine how far he has gone!

When we come to matters of faith, it is only natural that we face similiar problems of measurement. Many have tried unsuccessfully, for example, to prove the existence of God by natural reason.

An eleventh-century theologian and archbishop, Anselm of Canterbury, formulated the ontological argument to prove God's existence. Basically, he held that the very concept of a supreme and perfect being demands its existence. Twentieth-century philosophers, Norman Malcolm and Charles Hartshorne, continue the argument; but it has been decisively shattered. I could conceive of unicorns and mermaids, even perfect ones; but that does not demand their existence.

Thomas Aquinas, a thirteenth-century theologian, elaborately developed the cosmological argument for God's existence. The world's existence demands a cause. Every event demands a cause. A watch demands a watchmaker. But if so, who caused the event of God's existence? The argument breaks down.

The teleological argument of William Paley of the eighteenth century also falters. He was sure that intelligent design exhibited in the universe proves the existence of an intelligent Designer. But this would not prove that there is only one Designer, or that he is omnipotent, omniscient, and perfectly good.

Immanuel Kant's argument of God's existence from the postulate of moral law likewise runs into difficulty. Natural arguments can suggest, but not prove, God's existence. The world by wisdom can never arrive at God, the Apostle Paul proclaimed long ago (1 Corinthians 1:21). Jesus never tried to prove God's existence. He always assumed it.

Our inability to measure God does not negate His existence any more than our inability to measure love disproves the bond of affection between a husband and wife or between a parent and child.

In one of my doctoral courses, the philosophy of religion, the professor ridiculed any belief in a Supreme Being. "Blind faith," he sneered, "is incompatible with an intellectual approach to life." He told me about his father, a minister, and about the struggle he had gone through to liberate himself from his father's brainwashing. He was now an atheist, he declared, and had no more time for religious superstition than he had for the Easter bunny or Santa Claus.

In the discussion that followed, I suggested that he had only substituted one blind faith for another and that while there are no arguments that prove, there are also no arguments that disprove, a Supreme Power. He was now believing blindly that the six visible stars of the Pleiades in the constellation of Taurus, as well as the entire universe, was simply the result of a fortuitous concourse of spontaneous atoms. Someone has estimated that it would take 100,000 monkeys pecking on 100,000 typewriters, 100 million years to produce accurately just one play of Shakespeare. "It takes a lot of blind faith," I said, "to reject Genesis 1:1—'In the beginning God. . . .'"

Recently a girl said to me, "I reject all value systems."

I said, "You mean all but one—your value system in which all other value systems are rejected." Similarly, when we reject a theistic approach, we are burdened with a nontheistic approach.

This problem of observation and measurement is not limited to communication about God whom we cannot see. We are also inadequate when describing man whom we can see. Sure, we can say that man has 263 bones, 600 muscles, about 970 miles of blood vessels carrying about six quarts of blood . . . that the heart is a pump about the size of the fist that beats approximately 70 times a minute, 4,200 times an hour, 32,792,000 times a year . . . that our lung capacity is about 320 cubic inches with approximately 600 million cells breathing 2,400 cubic feet of air a day . . . and that each square inch of skin contains approximately 3,500 perspiration tubes each one-fourth inch long, making a total 201,155 feet, or nearly 40 miles (no wonder deodorants are so popular)!

Or we can say that the average man is approximately one-fourth ounce of iron, one-fifth ounce of sugar, 2 ounces of salt, 24 pounds of carbon, 10 gallons of water, a drop of iodine, 2 pounds of phosphorus, 112 cubic feet of oxygen, 7 pounds of lime, etc. No matter how many lists we could complete, our measurement would still be inadequate. All of our measurements, regardless of the discipline, are just approximations of reality.

When we are dealing with mathematics and engineering, our measurements and observations are sufficiently precise to construct skyscrapers and bridges or to thrust a manned vehicle into space. For example, the longest single span in the world to date is the 4,260-foot Verrazano Narrows Bridge at the entrance to New York harbor. This double-deck, 12-lane structure has riveted-steel towers 680 feet high carrying four main cables, each 36 inches in diameter, consisting of 142,500 miles of wires, which would stretch more than halfway to the moon. Because of the curvature of the earth's surface and the magnitude of the span, engineers had to design the tops of the vertical towers 1.6 inches further apart than the tower bases.

When dealing with matters of faith and theology, God and man, value systems and ideas, our task is much more arduous. God cannot be found at the end of a categorical syllogism. No chemical analysis can be made of the breath of God in a man (Genesis 2:7). Faith cannot be measured over a Bunsen burner. We have no serum or antitoxin to immunize us against false doctrine.

This does not mean that matters of faith are any less real; only that our measuring devices are inadequate. One way of coming into another person's world and demonstrating empathic understanding is to share common ground. Regardless of diverse or opposing views, we all share the common ground of measurement and observation limitation. Recognizing this limitation provides a fruitful climate for prayerful exploration. It also opens the door to the testimony of personal experience whereby we can invite a nonbeliever to take a leap of faith in expectation of a divine encounter.

THE CONTAINER MYTH

Sometimes we fail to come into the other person's world by unconsciously holding to a container myth regarding language. We speak and assume the other person must be really stupid or hard of hearing if he did not comprehend us. The container myth holds that words contain meaning much as a bottle contains soda. Our learning of vocabulary and our use of the dictionary add to the myth that there is meaning in words.

Actually, as we learned earlier, words have no meanings. Words are only marks on a piece of paper, vibrations in the air, or dots in a Braille card. Words are just symbols that evoke meanings in people. People have meanings and use words to express them. Words are a lot like maps. If I place my finger on a spot marking the confluence of the Schuylkill and Delaware Rivers, I say, "Here is Philadelphia." But, of course, no map is Philadelphia. No matter how detailed the cartography, no map can "contain" Philadelphia. Similarly, no matter how precise our vocabulary, words never "contain" meanings. It is imperative, therefore, that we come into another's world of perception by checking for understanding. If our message has not been accurately perceived, we must avoid an attitude of arrogance that results in impatience or chiding: "What's wrong? Are you deaf?" Rather, we should be glad to clarify our message and thus enhance understanding.

A first-grade Sunday school teacher asked her class to draw a picture of something she had talked about in the Bible lesson. Douglas drew a picture of an airplane occupied by three passengers.

"What's this?" the teacher asked.

"Oh, that's the Holy Family's flight into Egypt."

Linda became frightened in daily vacation Bible school. Suddenly she ran home as fast as her feet would carry her. "They want to wash me in the blood of a lamb," she explained.

While driving through the Ozarks of Missouri, I heard a radio preacher say: "I know I'm odd. I have my idiosyncrasies. At times I'm eccentric and unconventional. But God has called us to be a peculiar people."

What Douglas perceived as *flight* was not what the teacher meant by *flight*. Certainly no one was thinking of bathing Linda in blood. The biblical writers meant "chosen, special, precious, or unique" when the King James Version of 1611 used *peculiar*, a word that has changed in meaning over the years.

While the container myth is a barrier to all communication, it is especially a problem to Evangelical communication on the secular university campus. If a twentieth-century believer is to proclaim the biblical message to our time, he must convey that meaning in the world view and language of contemporary man. The pious phrases meaningful a generation ago are almost unknown in the secular world. Simply because *we* know what we mean does not guarantee that we are communicating to others. We show empathic understanding by coming into the other person's world of language.

Sometime ago I had dinner with Don Budge, one of the greatest tennis players of all time, who now spends several months each year teaching the game to others. He spoke to me recently about the problem of language in teaching. "I keep saying the same thing in as many ways as possible, hoping that something will register. I must keep reminding myself that the tennis jargon meaningful to tennis professionals does not communicate to the tennis novice." Don Budge knows a lot about tennis. He showed me he knows a lot about communication as well.

ACTIVE LISTENING

Another way we show empathic understanding is active listening. In fact, we often communicate more effectively by the way we listen than by the way we talk. Listening itself contributes substantially to a communicative climate. People open up to us and we make real sense in our communication only if we have adequately listened for both content and feelings.

Listening becomes effective to the degree that we move from passive to active involvement. Here are 14 rules for listening—seven do's and seven don'ts:

1. Maintain eye contact.

2. Sit or stand attentively.

3. React nonverbally by such gestures as a nod of the head and a warm smile.

4. React verbally by expressions such as "I understand" and "That's interesting."

5. React by asking questions that encourage a more in-depth analysis.

6. React by summarizing and demonstrating understanding of content.

7. React by expressions that demonstrate an understanding of feelings, emotion, and intensity communicated.

8. Avoid giving attention elsewhere, interrupting, looking at your watch, and edging away.

9. Avoid picking up on minor details rather than listening for the thrust of the message. It may be unimportant to the total meaning that in a particular sentence he misquoted a Scripture verse, substituted Peter for Paul, or was off by five percentage points on his statistics. Avoid correcting people in details, as well as pronunciation or grammar.

10. Don't be distracted by unusual mannerism or by gestures, repeated phrases ("You know?"), or malapropisms.

11. Avoid reacting to any particular idea until you have listened to the whole.

12. Avoid passing judgment on ideas. Get the person to pass judgment on his own ideas by restating them for him.

13. Avoid trying to change people. Behavior modification must come from within in light of new understanding.

14. Avoid argumentation and rebuttal, especially when the issue is not germane to the task at hand, expected performance, or church policy. Let the person talk. Listen for total meaning.

Many times it is more important to ignore content and to respond just to feelings. Suppose a worker says, "I'd like to melt down this machine and make paper clips out of it." Would it not be ridiculous to respond to content? Would it not be silly to speak of the economics involved and the price we would have to charge for those paper clips? Such a statement calls for an understanding of feelings: "I see you are having a rough day."

Suppose a child says to the mother, "You gave him a bigger piece of cake than you gave me." A response about the size of the cake would miss the point. The child is really asking for reassurance: "Do you love me as much as you love Tom?"

Suppose a choir director asks the pastor, "Just whose responsibility is the music room?" Answering such a question by content misses a great opportunity to listen empathically. A response to feelings would show far greater understanding. Such a response may be, "Do you feel that someone is challenging your authority?"

Remember that the most important aspect of listening is a demonstration of understanding. A person wants to know that he has been heard and that his feelings have been perceived. When emotions run high, feelings must be dealt with before constructive communication can proceed. It is far more effective to demonstrate such understanding than to give helpful advice. By listening, we say, "I'm interested in you as a person. Your problem is important to me. Your ideas are worth listening to. Even if I disagree with you, I respect your thoughts and feelings. I understand that they are valid for you. I care about you. You can always talk to me." Such listening presents a beautiful climate for communication. It allows us to come into the other person's world.

CONFLICT

Another way we create a communicative climate and demonstrate empathic understanding is the manner in which we handle anger and conflict. Each of us knows from personal experience that communication is not always composed of sugar and honey. Conflict, bitterness, disagreement, and anger are part of everyone's communicative experience. What can we do in these unpleasant situations?

One thing we can do is to take a positive approach to conflict. If two persons were to think exactly alike on every issue, one of them would be unnecessary. Conflict becomes unhealthy when it continues after a decision has been reached, thus hampering the implementation of positive action.

Another thing we can do is to recognize that feelings are not involuntary. In the midst of a heated discussion, we can pick up the phone and pleasantly accept an invitation to dinner, only to resume the hostilities voluntarily. You cannot make me angry unless I choose to be angry. *You* do not make me angry. Anger is *my* response to you, and *I* am responsible for it. I am responsible for how I react to you, whether friendly or hostile, accepting or rejecting, welcoming or threatening. Poor habits of response, allowing others to trigger my psychological sets, can throw me out of control. But in the final analysis, the feelings are mine; and I must own them. Conflict can be managed if I own my feelings and you own yours.

Third, we can turn conflict into mutual victory. It is not important that I win or that you win. Such victories are costly, leaving open wounds that fester and cause problems later. It is only important that the business wins, the home wins, or the church wins by our conflict. We never win by putting someone in his place, making him feel small, or threatening his self-concept. When someone is angry, it is sometimes frustration. More often, anger is saying, "I am a unique and precious person. Recognize my ideas and treat me with respect." Conflict becomes healthy when both or all sides win—when the best ideas of opposing factions are implemented. Each person can win because he is heard, and has had an opportunity to contribute to the success of the project or relationship.

Finally, we should approach conflict by resolving one issue at a time. Problems are easier to handle sequentially when each party agrees to address only the topic at hand. Two papers to write, it seems, are an insurmountable task together; yet dealing with them one at a time, the student can meet both assignments. This concept also means that each party avoids all unnecessary references to past performances, conflicts, or problems. The parent can resolve a conflict with a child more easily by sticking to the present issue than by adding the weight of a difficulty that happened three months ago. To the immediate problem of breaking curfew, it is unwise to add the carelessness of breaking the lamp last summer.

Empathic understanding is the key to conflict resolution. For conflict to be resolved, both parties must win. When conflict becomes a mutual exploration for a solution acceptable to both or all parties, communication becomes relaxed and fruitful.

Just as coming into another's world makes sense romantically, empathic understanding makes sense communicatively. Empathic understanding is essential to a communicative climate.

6

POSSIBILITY THINKING

We noted in Chapter 2 that a leader's positive mental attitude generates trust; that is, we tend to trust the leader, minister, or teacher who exudes enthusiasm, optimism, and faith in achieving the goals of the church or organization. We trust the leader whose ideas are bigger than our own. We trust the person who exhibits possibility thinking.

In the context of this chapter, we are saying that possibility thinking is an ingredient of communicative climate. It is exhausting, stressful, and defeating to work, preach, or teach in a negative climate. It is almost impossible to persuade, motivate, or inspire where the vocabulary is "I can't" or "It won't work here." Even Jesus himself could do little in Nazareth because of unbelief (Matthew 13:58).

WHAT POSSIBILITY THINKING IS NOT

1. Possibility thinking is not ignoring a serious problem hoping it will magically disappear. Untreated problems, like infectious sores, tend to fester and spread. Spouses cannot merely wish away marital problems. Executives cannot ignore with impunity the signals of organizational conflict. Ministers cannot, in the name of faith, play spiritual ostrich, burying their heads in the sand to escape discord, insufficient finances, or stunted growth. Problems must be faced squarely and solved. When dissension over who would be the greatest broke out among the disciples, Jesus called the Twelve immediately and mediated the dispute (Mark 9:33-35).

2. *Possibility thinking is not a substitute for thorough research, planning, organizing, delegating, promoting, or advertising.* Nor is it a substitute for a poor product or inferior service. Jesus made this clear in the stories of the barren fig tree, the tower-builder, the king who contemplated war, and the salt that had no taste (Luke 13:6; 14:28-35). Positive thinking is never a substitute for an inferior sermon, an unorganized visitation team, an unprepared Sunday school teacher, or any other program of the church. Positive thinking is never a substitute for the anointing of the Holy Spirit or genuine worship.

3. *Possibility thinking is never misrepresentation or deception.* The unscrupulous salesperson who gets so enthused over the used car he is selling that he lies about its condition cannot be excused on the basis of a healthy positive attitude. The person who claims to be healed in spite of verifiable evidence to the contrary is neither glorifying God nor standing on His Word. He is practicing self-deception and destroying his Christian witness. When God heals, the healing will pass the most thorough medical examination. A leading radio evangelist recently told of a man who was healed each time he was present with the evangelist, but lost his

healing each time he went home because of doubt. No record exists in Scripture where someone was healed only to lose that healing sometime later. Possibility thinking does not misrepresent the facts, shade the truth, or underestimate difficulty or obstacles. To be successful in the long run, possibility thinking must be totally honest and trustworthy.

4. Possibility thinking is not a belief that one's natural resources are sufficient for every problem. It is not faith in one's own strength, talents, or plans. That is presumption and pride. And the Bible says, "Pride goes before destruction, and a haughty spirit before a fall" (Proverbs 16:18). Jesus said that this kind of pride "defiles a man" (Mark 7:20-23). Likewise, faith and possibility thinking are never schemes or magic formulas whereby we can force, cajole, or wheedle God into approving and prospering plans conceived without His guidance.

WHAT POSSIBILITY THINKING IS

1. Foremost, possibility thinking is an indomitable faith in God. The more we understand about God, the more we realize that we need never accept defeat as final. Actually defeat has no permanent meaning for the Christian except to describe the inevitable destruction of evil. Never need a Christian reach a point of total failure or despair. No evil can triumph ultimately over goodness. No illness can permanently destroy health. Jesus declared that not even death, our worst enemy, can terminate life (John 11:26).

2. Possibility thinking is an affirmation of scriptural promises. "We know that in everything God works for good with those who love Him, who are called according to His purpose" (Romans 8:28). Jesus said, "Have faith in God. Truly, I say to you, whoever says to this mountain, 'Be taken up and cast into the sea' and does not doubt in his heart, but believes that what he says will come to pass, it will be done for him. Therefore I tell you, whatever you ask in prayer, believe that you receive it, and you will" (Mark 11:23, 24). "I came that [you] may have life, and have it abundantly" (John 10:10).

3. Possibility thinking is the recognition of God's presence and assistance regardless of the severity of the circumstances. "God is our refuge and strength, a very present help in trouble. Therefore we will not fear though the earth should change" (Psalm 46:1, 2). "Fear not, for I am with you" (Isaiah 43:5). "My mouth shall praise thee with joyful lips: when I remember thee upon my bed, and meditate on thee in the night watches. Because thou hast been my help, therefore in the shadow of thy wings will I rejoice" (Psalm 63:5-7, KJV). "A thousand may fall at your side, ten thousand at your right hand; but it will not come near you" (Psalm 91:7). "My help comes from the Lord. . . . He who keeps you will not slumber. The Lord will keep your going out and your coming in from this time forth and for evermore" (Psalm 121: 1-3, 8).

One night a man dreamed he was walking with the Lord in the sand along an ocean beach. Across the sky flashed scenes from his life. In most scenes he saw two sets of footprints in the sand, one belonging to him and the other to the Lord. Yet there were other scenes during the lowest and saddest times in his life in which there was only one set of footprints in the sand.

This really bothered the man, so he questioned the

Lord: "Lord, you promised that if I decided to follow You that You would never leave me nor forsake me. Yet during the difficult times of my life there was only one set of footprints. I don't understand why, when I needed You the most, You deserted me."

The Lord replied, "My precious Child, I would never abandon you. During your times of trial and suffering, when you saw only one set of footprints, it was then that I carried you."

4. *Possibility thinking is the realization of our incredible inner resources as Christians.* "I can do all things in him who strengthens me" (Philippians 4:13). We are either the master or the victim of our thinking. Our attitude, not our aptitude, is the chief determinant of our own success. Positive thinking is basic to all achievement. Our attitude determines our reaction to any situation. We create our environment for success or failure—mentally, emotionally, and physically by the attitudes we *choose* to hold. If we believe we can't, we can't. If we believe we can, we can.

Whatever we believe tends to be a self-fulfilling prophecy. Faith is a way of thinking that gets results. The faith spoken of in the Bible is a conviction based on eternal laws and principles written into the constitution of our minds and bodies. Faith is the fusion of our thoughts and feelings, of our minds and hearts to achieve some worthy purpose. Recognize that you are indeed the salt of the earth and the light of the world (Matthew 5:13, 14). As a Christian, you have incredible inner resources. Believe that God will use your talents.

5. *Possibility thinking is the diffusion of all hurts.* Hurts are an inescapable part of life. Jesus himself, could not escape the hurt of an unresponsive Jerusalem (Matthew 23:37; Luke 13:34). King David had to face

the rebellion and death of his son, Absalom (2 Samuel 18:33). The Prophet Hosea anguished over the unfaithfulness of his wife, Gomer (Chapter 3). The Prodigal Son reaped the hurt of his own wrong choices and actions (Luke 15:14-16). Leaders usually encounter a greater number and variety of hurts than experienced by their followers.

A leader's response to his hurts determines in part his degree of greatness and success. Even if we are unresponsible for the hurt, we are responsible if the hurt is prolonged and immobilizes us. Through the power of God we can diffuse any hurt and become more sensitive and effective because of it.

Negative thinking makes us bitter. Possibility thinking makes us better. Negative thinking rehearses the hurt, thereby nursing the hurt. Possibility thinking disperses the hurt, thereby reversing the hurt.

6. *Possibility thinking is the natural way of life.* Negative thinking is abnormal. Possibility thinking heals the body and mind. Negative thinking throws poisons into the body and sours the emotions. We are made for faith. Faith is our native land. When we breathe negative thinking, we are like a drowning man gasping for air. Faith is our natural air. God made us this way. Whether Christian or non-Christian we are subject to God's law of faith!

Possibility thinking is tranquillity; negative thinking, unrest. Possibility thinking relaxes us; negative thinking squeezes us with tension and pressure. Possibility thinking makes us cheerful, energetic, and enthusiastic; negative thinking leaves us gloomy, fatigued, and despondent. Possibility thinking brings clean, fresh emotions and constructive ideas. Negative thinking brings destructive, depressing emotions upsetting the mind. Protect yourself against doubt, hesitation, and reasons why something won't work or can't be done. Protect yourself against negative thinking as you would against deadly exhaust fumes in a closed garage. Refuse to breathe the deadly negative fumes of inferiority, insecurity, adversity, perplexity, anxiety, irritability, inability, and scarcity. Form a habit of thinking on what is lovely and of good report (Philippians 4:8).

There is a solution to every problem when we place our dreams in harmony with God's plan and purpose. With God all things are possible. God is omnipotent and knows no opposition. Boldly believe that God will supply all your needs (Philippians 4:19). Each Saturday, contemplate the pulpit or the Sunday school class with the verse, "Tomorrow the Lord will do wonders among you" (Joshua 3:5). Dare to ask, seek, and knock in faith and watch the doors of opportunity open before you (Matthew 7:7). "For it is God who is at work within you, giving you the will and the power to achieve his purposes" (Philippians 2:13, *Phillips*). "According to your faith be it done to you" (Matthew 9:29). "He who began a good work in you will bring it to completion" (Philippians 1:6). "He who sows bountifully will also reap bountifully" (2 Corinthians 9:6). "Bless the Lord, O my soul. . . . who forgives all your iniquity, who heals all your diseases. . . . who satisfies you with good as long as you live" (Psalm 103:1-5).

7. *Possibility thinking is performance.* Possibility thinking without positive action is as dead as faith without works (James 2:17). If you aim at nothing, you will succeed! If you fail to plan, you are planning to fail! To a large extent, possibility thinking

is setting goals, making a plan to reach those goals, and confidently expecting to achieve them.

THE CHOOSING OF A GOAL

First, to be successful a goal should be conceivable; that is, concrete, conceptual, specific, visual, explainable, and definable. A nebulous, ambiguous, hazy, vague, or confused goal neither inspires a leader nor arouses his followers.

Avoid a personal or organizational goal like "trying harder" or "doing better." Choose a definite goal, such as "I will learn to control my temper." Conceptualize it: "I will photograph my thoughts and feelings. I will record my tone of voice. I will rid myself of the negatives, such as anger, criticism, and irritability. I will think, speak, and act from the viewpoint of God's love and His compassion."

Second, a goal should be believable and achievable. An organizational goal is successful to the extent that you believe it and to the extent that you can sell that goal to your followers. An organizational goal must appear reasonable and realistic corresponding to the level of faith and resources of your constituency. A personal goal need only be believable and achievable to you. You can reach your spiritual and personality goals regardless of the skepticism around you.

Third, a goal should be controllable; that is, centered in the area of your authority and influence. An example of an uncontrollable goal is expecting to borrow money from a bank for church expansion at 6 percent when the going rate is 16 percent. A personal goal that relies solely on the response of one other person is another example of uncontrollability.

Last, a goal should be measurable. The more you can quantify your goals, the better you can determine your degree of success both at the end of the timetable and at all checkpoints along the way. Possibility thinking is a sequence of interdependent and interrelated steps: (1) the formulation of clear, concise objectives, (2) the development of realistic action for obtaining them, (3) the systematic monitoring of achievement and performance, and (4) the implementation of corrective actions to achieve the desired results. Key concepts in this process are goal-setting, action-planning, periodic progress reviews, and corrective action.

Never make your goal perfection. When perfection is your goal, it takes only one error to remove you from contention. Likewise, to achieve second or third place in a field of many is success not failure. Don't give up if you find yourself achieving only 90 percent of your goal. That would be as foolish as someone who fails one day on a diet saying, "I might as well go on an ice cream and cake binge." Losing nine pounds when your goal was ten is still success!

A goal then is an achievement you could be pursuing, a dream you could be launching, a project you could be starting, a decision you could be making, a possibility you could be exploring, an opportunity you could be grabbing, a problem you could be solving, an idea you could be implementing, and a plan you could be executing.

SUMMARY

We now have seen that possibility thinking is an ingredient of communicative climate. It is easy to communicate when positive attitudes prevail and difficult to communicate when negative attitudes rule our mind. A leader with positive attitudes inspires trust.

We have noted four things that possibility thinking is not:

1. It is not ignoring a serious problem hoping it will disappear.
2. It is not a substitute for positive action, a poor product, or inferior service.
3. It is never misrepresentation or deception.
4. It is not an exclusive reliance on one's own talent.

We have studied seven characteristics of possibility thinking:

1. It is an indomitable faith in God.
2. It is an affirmation of scriptural promises.
3. It is the recognition of God's presence and assistance regardless of trials and circumstances.
4. It is the realization of our incredible inner resources as Christians.
5. It is the diffusion of all hurts.
6. It is the natural way of life. Mankind is made for faith. Negative thinking can poison the body as well as the mind.
7. It generates the positive action of setting clear concise goals, developing a realistic plan for achievement, monitoring performances, and tak-

taking corrective measures to ensure results. Our goals should be conceivable, believable, achievable, controllable, and measurable. Finally, possibility thinkers achieve despite all obstacles.

Stop your fears before your fears stop you! "For God did not give us a spirit of timidity but a spirit of power and love and self-control" (2 Timothy 1:7). "You shall receive power when the Holy Spirit has come upon you" (Acts 1:8).

7

PROBLEM-SOLVING

We have seen that good communication is a set of skills indispensable to any interpersonal relationship whether between many or just two. Communicative skills are always related to process: providing a communicative climate, conveying and receiving information, persuading, motivating, inspiring, and proving effective leadership. We are now ready to consider another set of communicative skills—the process of solving problems.

The purpose of this chapter is to teach a set of skills that will enable you to help others deal more effectively with crisis, change, and stress. These skills also will help you solve the problems of your church more effectively. The techniques suggested here are based on a large body of communication research and upon the solid ground of Scripture. They have been proved effective.

THE INEVITABILITY OF PROBLEMS

Every person has problems. Every business has problems. Every church has problems. We will never arrive at a problem-free state of happiness in this life. Even the Garden of Eden presented the first couple with the problem of temptation (Genesis 3:1-19). Life is a journey, not a destination, and is filled with challenges to our tranquillity (Job 14:1).

The child often expresses the delusion that if he were an adult, all his problems would be solved. The adult sometimes expresses the delusion that if he could change job or spouse, somehow his life would be miraculously perfect. Since wherever we live or work we will face problems, it makes a lot of sense to learn communication skills to solve them.

Why are problems inevitable? For one thing God made us sensitive creatures. We can feel pain. This sensitivity is necessary to survive: to know that fire is hot, for example. But this sensitivity also allows us to anticipate pain or to relive our past suffering over and over again.

Another reason for the inevitability of problems is the fact of change. Life is not a static plateau to which we learn to adjust, but a dynamic journey of continuous change. Even the changes we want bring problems: marriage, children, a promotion, a new home, etc. The first step in problem-solving, therefore, is a recognition that problems are inherent to life. They are not enemies to escape or fear, but rather challenges to meet, face, and solve through the power of the risen Christ (Psalm 37:39).

THE SOLUTION TO PROBLEMS

While problems are inevitable, defeat is not. God is omniscient. He knows a solution to every one of our problems. We can align our thinking with God's knowledge and find our needed solution. Nothing is more pernicious to success than intense despair coupled with a belief that the situation is hopeless (2 Kings 6:15-17).

If I believe that defeat is inevitable, it is! If I believe that I am fighting a losing battle, I am! Nagging, gnawing doubt produces a self-fulfilling prophecy of failure.

On the other hand, if I believe that God has a solution to my problem, if I believe, "If God is for [me], who [can be] against [me]?" (Romans 8:31), what threatens from behind me and what stands as a roadblock before me are insignificant matters compared to the faith of God that lies within me. If I can say like Moses with the Egyptian army behind him and the Red Sea before him, "Fear not, stand firm, and see the salvation of the Lord, which he will work for you today" (Exodus 14:13), then victory is inevitable.

The second step in problem-solving is believing that God has a solution for us. Neither defeat nor despair are inevitable.

THE NATURE OF PROBLEMS

We can understand any problem better if we realize that all problems are feelings. This does not mean that our problem is not real, that it is psychosomatic, or that it is a figment of our imagination. It does mean that a personal problem is always a felt discrepancy between things as they are and things as we would like them to be.

Of course, a person can have a problem without realizing it. Generally speaking, however, it is a problem to someone else rather than to him. A question of my 10-year-old son to his mother is a case in point: "If my messy room is not bothering me, why is it bothering you?"

My wife replied, "Because it is a problem to me, I'm making it a problem for you. You may not go outside until your room is presentable."

Wanting to go outside, my son now felt the messy room was a problem.

The third step in problem-solving is a personal awareness of the problem. We do not correct that which we do not feel and see.

Worry and distress are not enemies in themselves. Only when we feel a problem are we moved to solve it. Some feeling of unhappiness is necessary, therefore, to problem-solving success. Some feeling of discontent must clamor for resolution before we take action.

THE CAUSE OF PROBLEMS

A cause is always what stands between existing conditions and desired conditions. A problem and its cause are current; that is, we cannot blame something in our past for our present dilemma.

To be sure, past events can have considerable impact on our present options. A young man's failure to graduate from college can close the door of many job opportunities. Notwithstanding, a problem is always something present; that is, the problem is always contemporary. "So, in light of all conditions and circumstances, past and present, what am I going to do now?" We cannot solve yesterday's problems. As adults, we cannot change our childhood. We cannot retrieve a lost loved one. But our problem and its cause are current. What do I do about the way I feel now?

We can generally identify one to three areas of a problem: a situation, a behavioral pattern, and a thought pattern. A cause can be one of these three things or a combination of two or three of these things.

Take a financial problem, for example. Its cause could be a situation. Perhaps Sam brings home a paltry paycheck, one with which any family of four would have a rough time surviving.

Or the cause could be a behavioral pattern. Sam and Cynthia spend more than Sam makes. The income could be adequate, but the spending is outrageous!

Or the problem could be a thought pattern. The income is adequate. Sam and Cynthia are living within their means, but they are unhappy about it. Sam would like to be driving a Cadillac instead of a Chevrolet, and Cynthia has her heart set on a $5,000 fur coat. Typically, a problem has a combination of causes.

What is a solution? We can now identify a solution as something that changes the situation, changes our behavior pattern, or changes our thought pattern.

Sam could change jobs to one with more pay. Cynthia could go to work. We could treat the situation. Or Sam and Cynthia could make a budget and start living within their income. Or both could change their thinking to more realistic expectations. Quite often a problem has more than one solution.

THE ELEMENTS OF A GOOD SOLUTION

1. *A solution is easier to execute when it involves a moderate change rather than a drastic one.* This means that a solution is more likely to succeed if you start with realistic, modest goals, which subsequently are gradually increased. Depending on your present state of physical fitness, it is easier to start with a goal of 30 push-ups than with 60 in a new exercise program.

2. *A solution is easier to achieve if you tackle only one major problem at a time.* Psychologically it is often wise to begin with your easiest problem first. The success of your first effort will give you a more positive attitude for a more difficult problem.

3. *A solution is always easier when you communicate positively about doing something rather than not doing something.* Suggesting the many places a child may ride his bicycle is more effective than just an enumeration of the forbidden territories. Emphasizing the starting of a jogging program can be more effective in helping a teen-ager give up smoking than just a negative goal of prohibition.

4. *A solution is easier when it has the support and encouragement of key persons.* For an individual sustaining a diet, the support of family members and friends is crucial. When launching a new church ministry, for example, it can be most effective to select key members to speak three to five minutes in its support for consecutive Sundays.

5. *A solution is easier to achieve when you can reinforce that achievement with an immediate reward.* A new dress may be a good reward for a woman who achieves the goal of a diet. A dollar for every *A* on a report card may be a good reward for a third-grader.

A victory dinner at the finest restaurant in town may be a good reward for visitation workers and their spouses who just canvassed 10,000 homes in your community. The reward should be known by all involved before the project is begun. We tend to repeat behaviors that reward us and to discontinue behaviors that sting us or give us no reward.

6. A solution is easier when the problem is fresh. Address church problems quickly. Detect and correct poor study habits early in a child's educational career.

7. A solution is easier when the problem is a specific situation, action, or thought pattern. Identifying a person as the problem usually exacerbates the difficulty and destroys a communicative climate.

8. A solution is easier when it is communicated in definite and specific terms rather than in vague generalities.

EIGHT STEPS TO SOLVING A PROBLEM THROUGH COMMUNICATION

Step 1. Identify and define the problem. If in this process you identify more than one problem, deal with each problem separately. It will be helpful to remember that a problem is a felt discrepancy between things as they are now and things as you would like them to be.

For personal problems, ask yourself, "How do I feel? hurt? frustrated? angry? hostile? fearful?" Be specific. "In what area do I feel this way? job? finances? marriage? a relationship at work?" Again, be specific.

Accurate information is essential to self-change. It is difficult to get directions for your life if you don't know where you are. If you should get lost on the way to a friend's house, and call that friend for directions, you will have to tell that friend exactly where you are or he will not be able to assist you.

Keep a diary of your feelings. Note the times, places, and people with you when this feeling occurs. Note the intensity of the feeling by assigning a number from one to ten. Note the duration of the feeling. Accurate information will help identify causes of your problem. It will help you suggest solutions to your problem. And accurate information is essential to evaluate future progress.

For your church or organization, you can best identify and define problems by measuring your church's performance against the criteria of your annual goals and objectives. Accurate record-keeping with each church ministry is essential to this process. Records communicate regression, stalemate, or progress.

Step 2. Identify and specify the causes of your problem. Make sure you specify a cause that is current and not some irreversible event in the past. Identify the causes in terms of a situation, a behavioral pattern (something you are doing) and a thought pattern (a way you are thinking or believing).

Suppose, for example, that a man's problem is one of anger and temper. You may help him identify the cause as a behavioral problem:

a. He tends to make mountains out of molehills.

b. He doesn't express feelings on a continuous basis, but instead allows feelings to build, while keeping score, until he explodes like a volcano.

You may further help identify the cause as a thought pattern:

a. He tends to perceive everyday problems as a personal insult. (A driver was insulting him when he accidentally cut him off in traffic.)

b. He erroneously believes that an "uncontrollable" temper relieves him of the responsibility for anger. (We are, of course, if not insane, responsible for all our actions and reactions.)

For a church organization, we may identify the major, minor, and related causes of a problem. We cannot take a single constructive step forward in any inquiry unless we analyze the causes for our dilemma. Our main focus throughout the process of identifying problems and their causes should be a search for new understanding. Looking to the same sources, asking the same questions, reflecting and comparing the information by the same criteria will perpetuate the status quo of unsatisfactory conditions. Such an inept process can be as much an obstacle to gathering and evaluating information as no process at all.

Causes should be identified as singular (one-time) or recurrent. The problem of a man laid off after 16 years of a solid work record is quite different from that of a man fired repeatedly from a dozen jobs over the last 10 years. Look at the A B C's to help identify causes. All behavior (B) is sandwiched between antecedents (A)—things that precede it—and consequences (C)—things that follow it.

Step 3. Specify a goal for improvement. Distinguish between continuous and one-time goals. Distinguish also between long-range and short-term goals. Short-term goals of up to eight weeks are better motivators than long-range distant goals of up to a year or more.

We have already noted in Chapter 6 that goals are most effective when conceivable (specific and graphic), achievable (realistic), believable (at your faith level), controllable (within your sphere of influence), and measurable in terms of numbers and quality. Goals and objectives are the vehicle for both individual and management planning.

While short-term goals usually provide better motivation, long-range goals are needed by both individuals and organizations. Long-range planning can be divided into five classifications for churches:

a. Physical planning. This deals with spatial needs—a parsonage, a bigger church nursery, more classroom space.

b. Process planning. This focuses on sequential operations of an organization such as a calendar of the year's events.

c. Human resource planning. This focuses on future staffing needs as well as training and developing your present staff of teachers and workers.

d. Functional planning. This is specific planning for organizational activities—planning for a revival, an Easter cantata, a radio broadcast.

e. Master planning. This integrates the other four types of planning into a coordinated and comprehensive framework to guide the organization.

Step 4. Establish criteria for a best solution. In deciding on a solution for a personal matter between husband and wife, the criteria may include fairness to both, something within a specific budget, something by consensus—acceptable to both. Criteria will differ according to the problem involved.

For a church problem, criteria for a best solution may include cost, extent of abilities and talent of personnel, ease of implementation, and other criteria depending on the nature of the problem.

Step 5. Brainstorm for solutions. Generate as many solutions to a problem as possible. Even foolish-sounding solutions are important here for something may be identified that can become part of the best solution. No attempt should be made at this stage to evaluate solutions. Evaluation at this time would inhibit a free response.

In a counseling situation try to get the person to generate his own solutions. In a church brainstorming session, encourage responses from everyone on your committee. Direct solutions to the three areas of problems: changes in the situation, changes in behavioral patterns, and changes in thought patterns.

Step 6. Choose the best solution. Narrow your solutions down to the best two or three. Then evaluate each solution by the criteria you established in Step 4. The best solution is the one that best satisfies your criteria. Sometimes your best solution may have several aspects that satisfy the different parts of a problem.

Step 7. Implement your solution. Decide who does what by when. For a personal problem, a solution should be tried for at least eight weeks. Usually it will take this long to evaluate your progress. Whether personal or organizational, accurate records should be kept to measure improvement.

Step 8. Evaluate your solution. At predetermined intervals measure your progress. Make any adjustments or refinements to ensure reaching your goal. Sometimes a solution will prove to be inadequate. Again we must look to the dynamics of the situation. A solution, although viable today, may become obsolete down the road. Feedback is the barometer by which we measure the revision process. If a solution becomes inadequate, start the problem-solving sequence over again. You can find a solution that will work.

At each stage of the problem-solving process it is important to seek the guidance of the Lord. With our own ingenuity we will fail, but with His guidance we will always succeed. After fishing all night, the disciples caught nothing. At the command of the risen Lord, they cast their nets on the right side of the boat. Obeying the command of Christ, the disciples could not haul in the load, for the catch was so great (John 21:1-6)! Christ has the answer to every problem. "In all thy ways acknowledge him, and he shall direct thy paths" (Proverbs 3:6, KJV).

THREE STEPS TO NEW THOUGHT PATTERNS

It is difficult for a man or woman, adult or child to change his thought patterns. Yet such a change is usually necessary in dealing with personal problems. If behavior alone is changed without a corresponding change in attitude, behavior tends to revert quickly to previous norms. The good counselor helps people to identify attitudinal problems. How we think about ourselves and our problem will determine how we feel and what we do about it (Proverbs 23:7, KJV).

The first step to changing beliefs is to identify them. What are our beliefs about ourselves? Few things are more detrimental than a negative self-image (Proverbs 3:26). What are our beliefs about our goals? A goal for improvement is easier to live with than a goal of perfection.

What do we believe about the roles we play in our

interpersonal relationships? The husband, for example, who expects his wife to wait on him hand and foot, after she has worked all day too, has some mistaken beliefs about her worth and his role (Colossians 3:19; Ephesians 5:25).

Sometimes the most pernicious belief of all is that of prejudiced perception; that is, people are often guilty of wearing problem-colored glasses. In every room of life they enter, things appear dark! They communicate failure and misery by face and voice.

The second step after identifying beliefs is to evaluate them. In a counseling situation, always strive to get the counselee to evaluate his own beliefs. This is a difficult step because everyone thinks his beliefs are correct.

Beliefs should be evaluated by at least three criteria: (1) Do they make sense? (2) Do they get us into trouble? (3) Do they agree with the Word of God? Suggest that a person play the role of an opposing attorney and deliberately punch holes into his own way of thinking.

The third step is to get a person to talk about alternative ways of viewing himself and his world. Compare the new beliefs to new clothes in a store. "Just try them on. You don't have to buy them if you don't like them." Challenge a person to wear his new beliefs for eight weeks and to act as though his beliefs were really true. Then, let him observe the difference—in himself and in his relationships.

SUMMARY

We have seen that communication skills are essential to the problem-solving process. Some problems are inevitable. Problems are not enemies to fear, but rather challenges to solve. Every problem is an opportunity. God has a solution to every problem. Neither defeat nor despair is inevitable.

We can generally identify one to three areas that cause our problems: (1) a situation, (2) a behavioral pattern, and (3) a thought pattern. A cause is always current. A solution is something that changes the situation, our behavior, or our thinking.

We have seen that a solution is easier when . . .

. . . it involves a moderate change.

. . . we tackle only one problem at a time.

. . . we emphasize the positive and downplay the negative.

. . . we enlist the support of key persons.

. . . we provide a reward or incentive for achievement.

. . . the problem is fresh.

. . . the problem is a situation, action, or thought as opposed to a person.

. . . it is definite and specific rather than vague and general.

The eight steps to solving a problem through communication are . . .

. . . identify and define the problem.

. . . identify and specify the causes of the problem.

. . . specify a goal for improvement.

. . . establish criteria for the best solution.

. . . brainstorm for solutions without evaluation.

. . . choose the best solution.

. . . implement the best solution.

. . . evaluate your progress.

The three steps for changing thought patterns are . . .

   . . . identify your beliefs.

   . . . evaluate your beliefs.

   . . . generate alternative ways of viewing yourself and your problem. Wear your new beliefs for a minimum of eight weeks and evaluate your progress.

8

LEADERSHIP PRINCIPLES

After a generation of phenomenal growth, Evangelicals now number 59 million in the United States and 157 million in the world. Without doubt Evangelicals have become the most active and vital force in global religion today, commanding a healthy majority of all Protestants. Leading this spectacular growth are the Pentecostals, who in 1982 comprised 39.5 percent of all Evangelicals: 51 million Evangelicals belong to Pentecostal denominations, while an additional 11 million members of other denominations follow Pentecostal practices.[1] By and large this dramatic expansion has been accelerated by unprecedented Evangelical and Charismatic leadership.

---

[1] *World Christian Encyclopedia*, ed. Dr. David B. Barrett (Oxford University Press, 1982).

Bill Bright, director of the successful Campus Crusade for Christ International, has embarked on what he describes as the most extensive Christian social and evangelistic mission in recorded history. Backed by Presbyterian billionaire Nelson Hunt, who heads the executive committee, and Baptist millionaire Wallace Johnson, campaign chairman, Bright expects to raise $1 billion in the next four years, to saturate the earth with the gospel. Johnson, of Holiday Inns, is traveling 20,000 miles a month lining up contributors. That's spiritual vision! That's leadership.

Pat Robertson founded the Christian Broadcasting Network (CBN). This Yale law school graduate purchased a satellite transmitter in 1977, the first to be owned by an independent TV producer. Today this satellite simultaneously feeds gospel programs to his four CBN channels and 130 other stations at an annual cost of $20 million. Robertson is the Johnny Carson of Christian TV, hosting the *700 Club*, viewed daily by millions. Each year the *700 Club* responds to over a million calls for spiritual help. In 1978 Robertson opened the first component of a proposed $50 million university and school of communications. Familiar with campaigning for his father, the late U.S. Senator Willis Robertson from Virginia, Pat campaigns nationally for Christ. That's leadership.

Billy Graham has preached to over 80 million persons globally, not to mention the audiences he has reached by TV. He has witnessed regularly to heads of state and has been called frequently for counsel by five of our Presidents. Beautifully he has blended show business and the gospel, using Christian celebrities to endorse the wonders of being born again. He initiated the World Evangelical Congress, which held its first meeting in Lausanne, Switzerland, in 1974. Approximately 8 million persons corresponded with Graham this year, donating about $30 million to help proclaim Christ. That's leadership.

In 1965 Oral Roberts opened a new university with a freshman class of 700 students. At a time when private colleges were beginning a struggle for survival, he dared to spend $1.5 million on the latest dial-access, audio-visual, computerized retrieval system to help professors teach and students to learn. Today the university has an enrollment of over 4,000 studying on a $100 million campus, with graduate study offered in six areas including law, business, and theology. In 1981 Roberts completed a $100 million hospital and medical school across the street from the 10,575-seat sports and TV arena and the 200-foot Prayer Tower. Approximately 60 million persons watch his variety TV specials in which he preaches a Charismatic message for the mind, body, and soul. That's leadership.

Like many a metropolis, the inner city of San Antonio, Texas, is decaying. Large churches are half-empty. Pictures on the bulletin board relate a history of past success followed by steady decline. First Baptist is a magnificent exception. Jimmy Allen, elected president of the Southern Baptist Convention in 1977, has increased membership in his church from 7,000 to 9,000 in the last decade. How? He has instituted some 20 ministries to meet inner-city needs; among them, an inn-restaurant where 55 volunteers always witness (without pressure) to paying customers. Profits are used to feed anyone who is hungry—free, no questions asked. A hotel serves the homeless. A street ministry trains young people to talk to troubled teenagers.

Over 1,000 Chicanos now claim First Baptist as their church home. That's leadership.

Paul Moore ministers to midtown Manhattan's Church of the Nazarene. He has bought the once-fashionable Lamb's Club in the theater district and transformed it into a Christian nightclub and restaurant with wholesome professional entertainment. It also houses a residence for young actors and artists and serves as an outreach to derelicts, runaways, and drug addicts. Noting the failure of government and humanistic traditional church programs, Moore in new ways calls for the transformation of lives by meeting Christ. That's leadership.

Whether it be Alexander the Great solving the mystery of the Gordian knot with one stroke of his sword, or the military genius Hannibal crossing the Alps on the absurd transportation of elephants, or Mahatma Gandhi shaking the yoke of colonial oppression through the contradiction of passive resistance, or Martin Luther defying the authority of the established ecclesiastical hierarchy, or Jesus himself with one Sermon on the Mount contradicting 2,000 years of sacred tradition (such as an eye for an eye and a tooth for a tooth), leaders have at least one thing in common: They see imaginative new ways to solve old problems. They understand the advice of Jesus that you cannot put new wine into old wine sacs (Matthew 9:17). They dare to be different. They dare to believe the unbelievable. They dare to perform the impossible.

MISCONCEPTIONS OF LEADERSHIP

A common misconception is that leaders do not make mistakes. We tend to build myths around our leaders. They become supermen and superwomen. We magnify their holiness until they are perfect. We exaggerate their wisdom until they are infallible. Yet, such a concept of leadership is foreign both to experience and to biblical example.

Moses was a great leader. He will be associated forever with the emancipation of Israel from slavery in Egypt. As long as the Passover is celebrated, Moses will be remembered as the leader of the Exodus. Was Moses perfect? No. In his youth he attempted to deliver Israel in a futile manner. Siding with an Israeli over an Egyptian would have caused Moses trouble enough; but to kill an Egyptian, that was political suicide as well as criminal homicide (Exodus 2:12-15)! Later in mature years when God commanded Moses to speak to the rock at Kadesh, did he not strike it twice? According to the biblical record this temper tantrum cost Moses the opportunity of leading Israel into the Promised Land (Numbers 20:12).

Moses was human. He made costly mistakes. Far from being infallible, leaders of any era make mistakes in perception, judgment, and action. We must always focus on the perfect God using the imperfect leader. We should never be surprised to discover feet of clay on legs of strong leadership.

Was David a leader? Unquestionably. Unlike Moses, David showed great promise in youth, evidenced by his fearless confrontation with Goliath (1 Samuel 17). Later as king of Israel he greatly extended the nation's boundary and raised much of the money for Solomon's Temple. Yet, who does not know the story of David and Bathsheba: adultery and murder (2 Samuel 11)?

What about the New Testament? How about the Spirit-filled leaders after Pentecost? These leaders were also human. Perhaps Paul should have taken Mark on his second missionary journey rather than break his friendship in a heated argument with Barnabas (Acts 15:36-39). Perhaps Paul might have been more charitable to the high priest Ananias (Acts 23:3). Peter mistakenly tried to force circumcision on Gentile converts of Christianity (Galatians 2:1-9).

Church history records the errors of great leaders. St. Augustine discovered too late that he had no need to castrate himself to be holy. John Calvin shamefully had Servetus burned at the stake for denying the Trinity. Martin Luther should not have called the Book of James "an epistle of straw." The Bible says, "Great men are not always wise" (Job 32:9, KJV). Franklin D. Roosevelt, the only man elected to our highest office four times, guessed that only 51 percent of his presidential decisions were the best options available to him. Like an investor, the more risks a leader takes, the greater the number of mistakes that will be made. Further, even the best decisions will be considered mistakes by some of the people.

M. J. Rathbone, past president of Exxon, says that a leader learns significantly more by mistakes than by successes. Earnest Breech, who held top positions with General Motors, Ford, and Trans World Airlines, sees the leader's greatest asset is the freedom to learn through his own mistakes. Leaders learn something new every day, and sometimes it is the knowledge that what they learned yesterday is wrong!

Another misconception is that leaders should have all the answers. No one would deny the leadership role of Ann Landers among advice columnists. The American people, in a poll by *World Almanac*, ranked Ann Landers as the most influential woman in the nation. Her advice column is read by 60 million persons every day. Yet at age 57, Ann Landers was divorced by her husband of 36 years so that he could marry an Englishwoman in her twenties.

Six years before the divorce, Ann had written about her husband Jules Lederer: "Thirty years with this unselfish, supportive responsive man have enabled me to live life as few people get to live it." After the divorce, Ann wrote: "The lady with all the answers didn't have the answer to this one." Psychologist Dr. Lee Salk, a noted authority on marriage and family, was divorced around the same time as Ann.

No one knows all the answers. A leader is not one who knows more than anybody else. Rather, he is one who can tap the necessary sources of wisdom in others. Henry Ford, the automotive genius, was once ridiculed in a court trial. The opposing attorney deliberately pointed out his lack of formal knowledge. Ford replied that with one push of a button he could get the answers to any question he needed to know. "I pay men to know those things," he said.

The leader rises above yesterday's mistakes. The leader forgives himself completely for yesterday's failure. The leader does not let a mistake make him fearful or indecisive. He does not worry after a decision—only before. He makes his best judgment with the information available. Then he implements that decision. Of course, feedback may indicate a number of modifications in the future because adaptation to change is a part of continued growth (Philippians 3:13).

Here is a third misconception: A leader should work harder at the same tasks as his subordinates and should be able to do the job better than any members of his team (Exodus 18:13-23). Studies show that leaders are more effective when performing leadership functions such as organizing, planning, coordinating, and delegating than when trying to outwork others at their tasks. Furthermore, with today's specialization, there are areas of expertise where subordinates know more and are more highly skilled than their managers and leaders. A church board member, whose area of expertise is banking, may know more about borrowing money than the pastor.

Jesus made no attempt to handle the sails or oars when crossing the Sea of Galilee. In fact, He went to sleep (Mark 4:38). Nor did Jesus help with rolling away the stone at the grave of Lazarus (John 11:39). Leadership studies indicate that success is getting people to work cooperatively together by delegating authority and responsibility to the maximum extent possible. No one man can be skillful in every task so the leader learns to use the skills and experience of a lot of people. This is especially true as churches grow, expanding their ministries and becoming more complex.

We have looked now at just a few examples of great leadership among Evangelicals in the United States. They all have at least one thing in common: they see imaginative new ways to solve old problems. They dare to be different. They dare to believe the unbelievable and to perform the impossible. We have also examined three misconceptions about leadership: (1) that leaders make no mistakes, (2) that leaders have all the answers, and (3) that leaders should outwork others at their tasks. We are now ready to answer the question: Are there certain traits or skills that leaders have in common?

TRAITS OF LEADERSHIP

It seems incredible, but the word *leadership* was not invented in the English language until around 1800. Then another century marched by before social scientists began a serious study of the phenomenon of leadership. By the end of the third quarter of this century, however, over 3,000 research studies had been conducted; and the research continues, making leadership one of the most investigated topics of history.[2] From 1900 to 1950 the research centered around the traits of leadership. The studies asked, "What characteristics make a successful leader?"

Although traits are difficult to pinpoint and even more difficult to measure, at least three traits, it appears, correlates with successful organizational leadership.

1. *Communication Skills.* The successful leader has the ability to articulate meaningful goals. He possesses the knack of creating the communicative climate of trust, love, warmth, provisionalism, empathic understanding, and positive thinking. Affably he avoids power plays and diminishes defensiveness in others while sharing his message. Adroitly he teaches, encourages, inspires, stimulates, motivates, and persuades others. His communication is interpersonal; that is, his language enhances the feelings of personal worth in others. He talks to colleagues and subordinates as people rather than as objects to further corporate or organizational gain. He addresses personnel as team

---

[2] A book giving a survey and review of leadership research through 1973 is Ralph M. Stogdill's *Handbook of Leadership* (New York: Free Press, 1974).

members rather than as men to be manipulated on an organizational chessboard. Generally, without these communicative skills, whether in a Christian or secular organization, a person never emerges as a leader.

2. *Intelligence.* A leader tends to be brighter, sharper, and more intelligent than the average person. He is more adept at analyzing problems, generating solutions, unraveling complex issues, and handling crises. The leader utilizes the expertise and knowledge of others often more skilled and intelligent than himself in achieving his goals. He trains and teaches the less skilled and less knowledgeable and inspires them to achieve higher goals. By and large a minister attracts few above his own educational level.

3. *Achievement.* A leader has a good 85-amp battery. He is a self-starter. He rarely needs jumper cables. He is nearly always motivated to accomplish something. Achievement is its own reward. While compensation is expected, it is secondary. As the leader reaches one goal, he aspires to new goals. He is driven to accept responsibility. His dependability grows out of his inward determination to succeed. He expects others around him to achieve.

Sometimes these qualities are obvious. From the moment of his conversion, the significant accomplishments of Saul of Tarsus were evident (Acts 9:1-7). Often, however, these qualities of leadership are latent and dormant. God often calls a person not for the qualities he possesses, but rather for the possibilities of what that person can become through the Holy Spirit. Who but Jesus would see a blustering fisherman as a rock (John 1:42)? Who would suspect that Amos the shepherd and dresser of sycamore trees would become a prophet proclaiming the judgment of the Lord (Amos 7:14)?

Many traits of leadership such as friendliness, tact, patience, enthusiasm, and sympathy are rather widely distributed in the general population. It is a myth that each and every job requires a particular set of talents. On the contrary, most jobs (except highly technical ones) can be accomplished in a variety of ways by people with diverse sets of capabilities. Furthermore, we are talking primarily about Christian leadership where prayer with faith can move mountains (Matthew 17:20).

We have seen now that leaders generally have at least three characteristics in common: (1) they possess communicative skills; (2) they are more intelligent than the average; and (3) they are self-motivated achievers. We are now ready to ask the question: What does a leader do?

FUNCTIONS OF LEADERSHIP

More rewarding than a study of the traits of leadership is an understanding of the acts and functions of leadership. Even while we were discussing the characteristics of communicative skills, intelligence, and achievement, we were talking more about function and activity than about inherent traits.

When we talk about communication, we are not talking exclusively or even primarily about a person possessing certain skills. We are talking more about a relationship between people. Under this concept, we are talking about leadership as a function of articulating group goals. It is a function of establishing a climate of such elements as trust, love, understanding, provisionalism, and positive thinking. It is the act of informing, teaching, encouraging, stimulating, motivating, and persuading. It is the function of promoting interaction, cooperation, need satisfaction, and group maturity. It is the act of providing social support and exemplary behavior. It is the act of protecting individual rights, arbitrating conflicts, defining problems, and generating solutions. And most people can be taught to do these things!

Likewise, when we talk about the trait of intelligence, we are talking about applied intelligence. Some of the most ignorant persons I have met have Ph.D.'s! Intelligence must be applied to the functions of formulating goals, tasks, and objectives. It must be applied to the acts of planning, evaluating, coordinating, clarifying, integrating, and delegating. Again, most people can be taught to do these things!

Similarly, when we talk about the trait of achievement, we are talking primarily about the act of doing something. We are talking about establishing goals and objectives and reaching them. We are talking about accomplishment: starting a bus ministry, initiating a professional counseling center, developing a drug program for youth, beginning a television ministry, raising the budget for a new church edifice, starting a Christian nightclub, opening a Christian restaurant where waitresses witness to paying customers, conducting a positive-thinking rally, teaching a Sunday school class, winning souls to the Lord on the visitation team, providing a Christian day care center, commencing a Christian dating service, operating a Christian employment agency, or staffing a Christian school. The list is endless!

The question of "What is there to do?" is too broad. It staggers the imagination. The proper question is, "What can *I* do?" To that there is an answer. Every Christian can learn to be an achiever. Every Christian can accomplish something for God.

What I have described as the functions of leadership answers the pervasive question of whether a leader should be human relations-oriented and person-centered, or whether a leader should be task-oriented. Clearly, the answer is that the effective leader must be both a human-relations specialist and a task specialist. Human relations without goals and tasks is equal to faith without works—and just as dead. On the other hand, successful leaders realize that they can accomplish God's work only through people. People must always be treated with dignity and respect. They also need to be motivated. It is the leader's role to unite and stimulate followers toward specifically defined objectives in a warm and hospitable environment. The most successful churches are those whose churchgoing has been expanded to daily involvement, where sometimes hundreds of lay persons direct and assist in special ministries.

STYLES OF LEADERSHIP

How a person attempts to lead usually determines the degree of success or failure. A leader can have sound objectives and worthy goals thwarted by an inappropriate leadership style. Nowhere do we communicate more forcefully either favorably or unfavorably than by the way we attempt to lead.

Many styles of leadership have been stereotyped in research literature. Rarely does a leader's behavior consistently operate within any one classification. We will look at five styles, noting some advantages and liabilities of each.

Authoritarian Leadership

Typical of leadership from the Industrial Revolution to the 1940s is the authoritarian style. This is the style represented by Theory X stereotyped by Douglas MacGregor in his 1960 book *The Human Side of Enterprise*. This style is still practiced widely in businesses and churches, especially those wrapped around one founder.

At its worst, this style represents the autocrat who makes all the decisions, however trivial, and who parcels to each member daily assignments in minute detail. Because information is power, he withholds important data necessary in decision-making. Believing that all members are inherently lazy and untrustworthy, he tells subordinates what to do, and how and when to do it. His way is the only way. He is always right.

The authoritarian leader is not interested in feedback or upward communication. When he says, "Jump," he expects the subordinate to ask, "How high?" on the way up. This person is highly opinionated, dogmatic, and unchangeable. He keeps workers in constant competition for his favors. He substitutes authority for persuasion, and control for motivation. He often tries to lead by psychologically hitting people over the head. But that's assault, not leadership.

In some cases the authoritarian leader is paternalistic, making what he considers to be the best decision for those under him. But he still makes all major decisions, and his way of doing something is the only acceptable way.

The authoritarian style of leadership is most effective when . . .

. . . *there is severe crisis.* At a time of crisis, someone must bring order from chaos.

. . . *certain inviolate policies are ignored, such as with financial affairs.* This is one area that calls for a firm policy with autocratic enforcement if the leader is to avoid future headaches. Any policy that violates Federal or state law must be dealt with firmly and unequivocally, such as may arise with selling church bonds and debentures.

. . . *disciplinary action is necessary.* If a person accepts employment, it may be clearly understood that he will refrain from smoking and from drinking alcoholic beverages. Such are the rules at Lee College or Wheaton College. The rules are clear, and no exceptions will be tolerated. With violation of these rules, employment will be terminated. Likewise, a pastor would have to remove a church leader from office who was discovered violating organizational standards.

. . . *a person is a novice and cannot conceptualize his job description.* A person who cannot swim should not be pushed into the deep end of the pool to drown! He must first be taught in shallow water before given freedom to explore the depths.

. . . *there is an emergency or when there is no time for lengthy participative deliberations.* Similarly, if the decision is trivial or routine, and is not worth the time of others, unilateral decision-making is effective.

. . . *the matter is part of the job description.* Decisions naturally rest on the shoulders of the one involved. The president or director or minister quite properly makes his own appointments, schedules, and itineraries.

. . . *the leadership position is powerful and totally accepted by all.* An example might be a commander in the armed forces.

. . . *the task is relatively simple and structured.* A production foreman cannot operate like a college dean.

. . . *the relationship between leader and members is strong.* A command becomes the battle cry for some cause or purpose with dedicated followers; for example, a minister instituting a new church ministry.

The authoritarian style of leadership is least appropriate when . . .

. . . *your staff is experienced and capable.*

. . . *teamwork and cooperation are essential.*

. . . *attitude change is desirable.*

. . . *there is time to generate productive thinking from a responsible group such as a church board.*

. . . *your staff is highly productive and most departments are performing efficiently.*

. . . *you wish to put some new program into operation.*

. . . *those working with you are volunteers without pay.*

When authoritarian leadership is one's predominant style, that leadership is generally negative and dysfunctional. Morale is low. Turnover is high. In a business, subordinates spend valuable time protecting themselves before every move. Useless documentation for even trivial decisions, needless memoranda, and files of unnecessary statistics are kept for post-mortem checks to prove that any mistake was someone else's fault.

The authoritarian style, on the whole, produces disinterested members who lack initiative because of little opportunity to develop their own abilities. Members withhold valuable ideas because they feel their leaders do not listen. Rumor tends to be rampant and destructive as members form informal alliances against what they perceive as repressive leadership.

Consultative Leadership

The consultative leader reserves the right to make all final decisions, but asks his staff for their ideas and suggestions before making up his mind. On minor matters and within job descriptions, he may allow a great deal of freedom and decision-making by his subordinates. Communication flows both upward and downward because members at all levels feel free to discuss job matters. Because the leader is willing to listen, he generates respect, cooperation, warmth, and friendship. Because he does listen, he refrains from going against majority opinion. He seldom rocks the boat. He rarely commits dramatic blunders. And he seeks a balance between task and membership needs.

Consultative leadership can be most effective when . . .

. . . *the staff is well trained and experienced.*

. . . *the various departments work well as a team.*

. . . *the goals and the objectives to reach those goals are shared by both leader and staff.*

Consultative leadership is inappropriate when . . .

. . . *the staff is untrained and inexperienced.*

. . . *there is dissension and disagreement over goals and objectives.*

. . . *initiating dramatic changes or new programs.*

. . . *teamwork is poor and esprit de corps is missing.*

Participative Leadership

A leader is successful to the extent that his subordinates are strong and effective. Participative leadership builds on this principle. Therefore, under participative leadership, decision-making is spread throughout the various levels of the organization. Participation by subordinates in organizational growth and development is maximized. The leader stresses optimal commitment to both the task at hand and interpersonal relationships. Communication is promoted assiduously through upward, downward, and lateral channels, and through an active open-door and open-mind policy.

Understood correctly, this is not a style in which the leader is passive or defers to majority rule. Rather, it is a dynamic style in which he invites his team to share with him in a wide range of decisions. Team members assist in defining the problem and generating a solution until a consensus is reached that satisfies both the leader and the team. The key is to stay at the negotiating table until a solution is generated that is acceptable to all.

The research data suggests that this style of leadership usually generates the highest level of achievement. It also fosters devotion by members of a group for one another, loyalty toward their leader, and commitment to organizational goals and objectives.

Participative leadership is most effective when . . .

. . . there is adequate time to participate before action must be taken.

. . . team members are interested in the topic, rather than regarding the assignment as unnecessary busywork.

. . . the value that comes from participation is worth

the financial cost involved. This is a judgment each leader must make.

. . . *the team members have the expertise and information to contribute intelligently.* If members are not knowledgeable and there is insufficient time to acquaint them adequately with the salient facts, participation becomes a meaningless pooling of ignorance.

. . . *participants speak the same technical language and understand what each other is saying.*

. . . *a communicative climate can be established, allowing for openness, a minimum of defensiveness, and an absence of retaliation.*

. . . *the decision-making authority lies within the participant's job description.* Sometimes a leader can ask for help with the understanding that the final solution will rest with the leader or with a higher echelon of management of which he is part.

. . . *the leader desires members of his organization to be more identified with organizational goals and objectives.* Those who participate are more committed and involved, and begin to speak of the organization as "we" rather than "they."

. . . *it is expedient that members learn from each other and absorb the complexities of the organization.* Participation is the best kind of staff development and leadership training. A management team provides the opportunity for the leader to exemplify the kind of leadership he wants the group members to use with their subordinates. In this way, effective leadership descends through the various levels of an organization or church.

. . . *high morale is important.* Participation helps satisfy the needs of belonging, self-esteem, and self-actualization—the strongest of needs in our society.

. . . high-quality decisions are imperative. Participation allows the leader to tap the full resources of his staff, for as research shows, group decisions are superior to individual decisions. Each team member is given an opportunity to initiate and to create, and in this way participation differs from consultation. Under consultative leadership group members are free only to suggest, but under participative leadership they are free to act.

Participative leadership is least effective when . . .

. . . a decision is needed quickly.

. . . there is a crisis, chaos, or an emergency.

. . . the issue is not worth the cost involved. Six persons deliberating two hours can easily cost $150, even with the relatively low salaries paid in religious organizations. Will the group produce a decision to justify the added cost?

. . . the group is large in number. Group effectiveness is ideal with five members and diminishes rapidly with more than seven participants.

. . . the topic is unrelated to the work assignment or interest of the participants.

Free-rein Leadership

At the extreme passive end of the scale is free-rein or substantive leadership. Here the leader allows experts under him almost complete freedom. The president of a college, for example, may leave most of the academic matters to his vice-president for academic affairs, and most of the financial matters to his vice-president for business affairs. The president helps the experts under him to achieve their goals with a minimum of control. For example, the president may be the chief fund-raiser for the university. Without these funds the vice-president for business affairs would have little to manage! Likewise a pastor may give an experienced minister of education a free rein.

Free-rein leadership is effective only when . . .

. . . *true experts head each area under the leader.*

. . . *these experts are performing well and making decisions that benefit the entire organization.*

. . . *these experts utilize participation as their dominant style of leadership.*

Free-rein leadership is ineffective when . . .

. . . *your staff is relatively inexperienced.*

. . . *the organization faces a time of chaos or crisis.*

Situational Leadership

Perhaps at this point you are feeling somewhat confused. Having looked at the scale of leadership styles from the most rigid task-oriented to the most passive human relations-oriented, you see that no one style is best in every situation. Similar positions can be performed successfully using different styles of leadership. Stylistic success depends upon five factors: (1) the situation, (2) the task structure, (3) the leader-member relations, (4) leader position power, and (5) the amount of experience and the degree of talent among the staff.

Let us look at each factor.

1. If the situation is one of chaos, strong autocratic leadership is necessary to restore order. A church that has just been divided needs firm leadership. A solid well-organized church staffed with experienced people should run more efficiently with participative leadership.

2. Task structure refers to the degree to which one specific way is required to do the job. A foreman's

role on an assembly line differs vastly from that of middle- and upper-level management. Most church programs lend themselves to a high degree of creativity allowing many options to fulfill their goals. Participative leadership is, therefore, most effective under this criterion.

3. Leader-member relations are determined by the degree of leader acceptance. Where there is group friction with the leader, reluctant compliance, or total rejection, leader-member relations are obviously low. A minister who has received an almost unanimous vote can occasionally use autocratic leadership on selected crucial issues and have it perceived as strong dynamic leadership. In contrast, the minister who has barely received a majority vote may be perceived as bullheaded and dictatorial by those who did not vote for him. The lesser the mandate to lead, the more consensus, compromise, and conciliation are needed for successful participative leadership. A founding father may have exceptional rapport with his congregation and be able to lead more firmly than a newcomer just out of seminary who has to earn his wings (1 Kings 12:1-15).

4. Position power primarily refers to the authority of the office. An overseer can sometimes say things a pastor cannot. An associate pastor or minister of education should always support the program of the senior minister. Subordinates can differ with the senior minister in private conferences with him while deliberations are still taking place. Once a stand has been taken, however, it is imperative that all ministers become "eager to maintain the unity of the Spirit" (Ephesians 4:3; Psalm 103).

5. If a minister is blessed with experienced and

talented workers, an autocratic style is most inappropriate. Participative leadership would be the norm while selected subordinates might be given a de facto (but not de jure) free rein. Novices, on the other hand, need careful direction (1 Timothy 3:6). "Let them also be tested first; then if they prove themselves blameless let them serve" (1 Timothy 3:10).

Within the same organization, situations vary and so should the style of leadership. Situational leadership, therefore, adapts to individual needs and changing circumstances, and hence is the most effective style of leadership. No leadership style solves all problems. There are some problems that have no feasible solution. Survival often depends on the ability to sustain tension without fight, fright, or flight.

Learning the techniques of managing others is one thing. Putting the principles of situational leadership into practice is something else. Effective leaders make a habit of good leadership. This requires a conscious, deliberate effort. Once mastered, good habits of leadership become a powerful ally.

When we learn a new management technique, we should immediately set out to make it a habit—an instinctive, ingrained part of our everyday actions. Consider, for example, a principle of management we learned in Chapter 4: suspending judgment until you have heard both or all sides of a question. Master this principle. Practice it religiously until it becomes a habit. The more principles we master and make habitual, the more effective leaders we become.

Every time we repeat a good practice, we reinforce and strengthen the habit. Exceptions weaken the habit. Only the steady practice of good leadership habits will make them a part of us.

One way to make good leadership principles a habit is to anticipate situations in advance. As you anticipate, practice or rehearse how you will handle the problem. I do not like the adage: "Never cross a bridge until you come to it." Success belongs to the men and women who can cross bridges in their imagination miles in advance of the procession.

A good style of leadership creates good will and high morale. Good will and high morale are two of the few products that your competition can never undersell. Remember that running any organization successfully is about 95-percent effective communication with people and only 5-percent economics.

SUMMARY

We have seen that leaders in all types of endeavors have one thing in common: They do the impossible. They believe the unbelievable. They achieve the unachievable. They think big thoughts and dream great dreams.

The leader achieves despite all obstacles.

We have seen some misconceptions of leadership: (a) that a leader never makes mistakes, (b) that a leader has all the answers, and (c) that a leader outworks others at their assigned tasks.

We have seen that leaders have at least three traits in common: (a) They tend to have good communicative skills to persuade and motivate others toward organizational goals and objectives. (b) They tend to be more intelligent than the average person. (c) They are self-motivated; they are achievers.

We have seen how to develop a psychologically

effective style of leadership and how we communicate favorably or unfavorably by the style we choose. As a predominant style, participative leadership is more effective than authoritarian, consultative, and free-rein leadership. Ideally, situational leadership should be our goal, in which we adjust our style depending upon five factors: (a) the situation, (b) the task structure, (c) the leader-member relations, (d) the leader's position of power, and (e) the experience and talent of one's staff.

We have seen that good leadership must be made a habit to be effective. Good technique must be instinctive and an ingrained part of our everyday lives. One exception, such as losing our temper, can destroy months of previous work at creating a communicative climate. By anticipating future situations, we can plan and rehearse an effective leadership style. We can cross our bridges before we come to them.

We are now ready to examine the aspect of power and motivation. An understanding of these principles is indispensable to a study of leadership communication.

9

POWER AND MOTIVATION

I have found that top-level management will pay more for the ability to deal with people than any other ability. The overwhelming majority of executives who fail in their jobs do so not because they lack expertise in their field, but because they have not learned to deal with people.

Being appointed a leader does not make one a leader. A leader can lead only if he or she has followers. Leadership can be compared to the role of the teacher. Being appointed a teacher does not make one a teacher. A teacher can teach only if he or she has learners. Learning is an interaction between teacher and pupil, regardless of the subject matter. In the final analysis, it is the pupil who accepts or rejects the instruction of the teacher. Similarly, leadership is an interaction between leaders and followers. In the final analysis, it is the follower who accepts or rejects the influence of the leader.

Leaders do not automatically get the respect and acceptance of their followers. Some specific skills are required. We will examine the basics of several key skills, but perhaps the most important skill is the use of power. Leaders succeed or fail, for the most part, by their understanding and application of power.

WHAT IS POWER?

Whatever else organizations may be, they are sociological and political structures. This means that organizations, religious or otherwise, operate by distributing authority and setting a stage for the exercise of power.

For clarity, let us identify and distinguish five kinds of organizational power worth our attention: (1) punitive or coercive power, (2) reward power, (3) positional power, (4) expert power, and (5) charismatic power. Power of any of these five kinds may be simply defined as the ability to influence the behavior of others. In a larger sense, power is the ability to influence the direction of the organization, both in its daily activities and in its long-range destiny. But power to influence an organization is again the ability to influence the behavior of individuals in that organization.

Punitive or Coercive Power

Punitive or coercive power is the means to force another person either to comply with your wishes or to face punishment. With the parent over the small child, the punishment could be physical. In an organization, the punishment is generally psychological. It is the power to deprive another of position, authority, advancement, career objectives, raises, bonuses, favorable assignments, status, recognition, staff assistance, equipment, office space, or even the job itself. "If you can't do the job," says the boss, "I'll find someone who can."

Let us say that you want to get Rover, the dog, to move, but Rover does not want to move. One way you could get Rover to move would be to kick him. Thereafter, when Rover sees you coming, he will move to avoid the pain. For an organization punitive power is a psychological kick to coerce a person to do something he would not otherwise do to avoid the deprivation of something he needs or wants.

Notice that fear plays a large part with coercive power. Rover fears the kick. It is thought that a kick must be used periodically, or the dog will lose his fear—and compliance. Similarly, the existence of a leader's punitive power is seen through its use. The more frequently it is used, the greater the fear of subordinates. Some time ago in one of my management seminars a president of a medium-sized corporation said, "There is nothing wrong with my organization that a few firings won't cure. You have to fire people periodically just to make others comply." Fear is intrinsic to punitive power.

Dependency is also a part of punitive power. The subordinate must be fairly dependent upon the leader to have his needs met, or if he feels abused, he will eventually get his needs met elsewhere. "You can't fire me," he says, "because ten minutes ago I quit." He then markets his skills to another organization. In a time of high unemployment, or if a person's skills are not readily marketable elsewhere, or if one's retirement income would be denied or significantly reduced, dependency and compliance could be great.

It is the use or threat of punitive power that causes

the most problems between leaders and subordinates. We will talk more about the use of punitive power and its effects, but first let us examine the other types of power.

Reward Power

This is the ability of the leader to remunerate someone financially or psychologically for compliance with his wishes. It is the positive side of coercive power. Again we can use the analogy of Rover, the dog. Rover still does not wish to move. But this time we do not kick Rover. Instead, we hold a bone in front of him. Rover moves to get the bone. Each time we want Rover to move, we must hold another bone in front of him. Similarly, you can charge a man's battery, and recharge it again and again. But this is not motivation. Only when the man has his own generator that adequately charges his own battery can we speak of motivation.

With this concept of motivation, we can examine some of the attempts of business to use reward power. One attempt has been the reduction of work hours. We have tried to get people to work more by letting them work less. For many, the four-day work week is here. From a six-day, twelve-hour-a-day work week at the beginning of this century, we are on our way to the six-day weekend. While we can rejoice in some of these changes, motivation inspires a person to work more hours, not fewer hours.

Spiraling wages and fringe benefits have been another attempt at motivation. The average fringe-benefit package now equals one-fourth of wages, and wages are rising faster than productivity. Have we motivated people? Yes, to seek higher wages and greater benefits, but not to do more or better work.

Psychological studies show that money is usually a poor motivator. It is a satisfier much more than a motivator. This means that compensation falls into the category of environmental factors such as company policy and administration, supervision, relationships with supervisor and peers, or working conditions in general. Compensation must be adequate for the work performed in light of what your competition is paying, or your organization is one in trouble. Without adequate compensation and environmental factors, you can expect strong discontentment. But with them, you have only no discontentment. You still do not have motivation.

In its motivational form, reward power is more psychological than monetary. It is the ability to reward people interpersonally by satisfying their emotional needs for belonging, identification, acceptance, warmth, responsibility, advancement, opportunity for personal growth, job enrichment, recognition, self-actualization, and achievement. These aspects of reward power lend themselves beautifully to all types of Christian organizations, especially those dependent upon volunteer service.

To achieve positive reward motivation, Frederick Herzberg's concept of job enrichment is applicable to many religious organizations. It would involve providing job freedom by granting authority to an employee in his activity; retaining some control while increasing accountability for his own work; introducing with adequate training new and more difficult tasks not previously handled; assigning individuals specialized tasks enabling them to become experts; and when possible, giving a person a complete natural unit of work such as a module, area, department, or division.[1]

Positional Power

Positional power is the traditional authority associated with one's formal position in an organization. The military notion of saluting the uniform rather than the man is part of this power concept. The vice-president, manager, or senior minister, because of his position, is perceived by subordinates to have legitimate authority to handle his responsibilities.

The exercise of this power is seldom a problem for the leader. There is no problem when the captain of the airplane says to the copilot, "Flaps down." The secretary gets her notebook when the boss says, "Take a letter." Likewise, the overseer or pastor can exercise the power inherent in his job description generally without difficulty (Acts 20:27, 28).

More and more, however, positional power is dependent upon expert and charismatic power. One must earn power; one must earn influence; one must earn leadership. Positional power is initially granted, but it is also quickly tested. If competence is lacking, positional authority is discounted more readily than ever before (1 Timothy 5:17).

Naturally, the higher the position, the more power is associated with it. Sometimes, however, a position that has no authority in its own right wields con-

---

[1] Frederick Herzberg, "One More Time: How Do You Motivate Employees?" *Harvard Business Review* (January-February, 1968), pp. 53-62.

siderable power. An assistant or secretary to the president is often such a person in an organization because he or she controls the access to power.

Expert Power

This power is generated from the special knowledge or expertise regarded as valuable in satisfying individual and organizational needs. Persons often become leaders initially by rising to the top on the basis of expertise in some area. The vice-president of marketing may have started as a salesman. Outselling his peers, he rose to district sales manager, then regional sales manager. Being able to lead his region to the best national record, he became the vice-president. The many plaques on the office wall for past achievement carry the message of expert power. Similarly, the head of a religious organization may have distinguished himself first as a pastor and/or evangelist before being named to a top administrative position.

In his role behavior, a leader exercises three types of expert power—technical, interpersonal, and conceptual. A leader begins by distinguishing himself in technical and interpersonal skills. As he is promoted to higher responsibilities, his technical skills become proportionately less important. Also, as he is promoted through the ranks, the leader becomes more dependent upon the technical expertise of others, especially his staff members. His continued success depends upon the experts he chooses to advise and assist him, and upon his interpersonal and conceptual skills.

A typical illustration from the Old West will further clarify the importance of expert power. The head of the U.S. Cavalry post was, of course, the colonel.

He had it all: the prettiest wife, the biggest house, the fastest horse, the crispest uniform; and he could tell everyone else on the post what to do. He possessed the pinnacle of positional power. He rose to the rank of colonel by distinguishing himself earlier in the Civil War. Now he was responsible for making the West secure by killing Indians who would not give up their land peaceably.

The colonel was the authority. His power was not challenged by the EEOC (Equal Employment Opportunity Commission), or ERISA (Employee Retirement Information Security Act), or OSHA (Occupational Safety and Health Administration), or the bargaining units of the AFL-CIO (American Federation of Labor and Congress of Industrial Organizations).

But who was really the one in control? Not the colonel. It was the scout. He wasn't married. He slept in a bunkhouse or tent. His horse was poorly groomed. His clothes were wrinkled. He was definitely staff. He had no authority over anyone. But the scout was the one in control. Why? Because only he knew the terrain, where the water holes were, and what the Indians were up to by their smoke signals and dances. The important information resided in the staff—the scout!

Of course, the colonel could fire the scout, but not without great risk and danger. So the colonel settled for authority, accountability, and responsibility. Similarly, in any organization, secular or religious, success of mission and objectives resides, in large part, in the expertise of key personnel, often in staff rather than line positions. Due to the sophistication of modern information systems, data-processing personnel are often those in key positions of expert power and control.

Charismatic Power

This power comes from the quality of leadership that inspires the personal devotion of large numbers of people. It is the power of personal magnetism, which inspires followers to identify with both the leader and his cause. Charismatic power is often essential during the birth period of an organization. Here the magnetic or dynamic personality serves as a rallying point for the conception and a catalyst for the direction of the enterprise.

Oral Roberts, Billy Graham, Robert Schuller, Jerry Falwell, Rex Humbard, and Pat Robertson are but a few of the many ministers whose personal charisma has given birth and direction to religious organizations. Sometimes leaders inspire devotion to unworthy causes and pernicious cults. Such was Jim Jones, who, in 1978, turned an idyllic dream into a hellish nightmare as he led some 900 members in a ritual of mass suicide and murder in Jonestown, Guyana.

POWER THAT GETS US INTO TROUBLE

We have looked at five kinds of power—punitive, reward, positional, expert, and charismatic. The first of these—punitive power—the power to coerce and control—can get us into trouble in dealing with people.

Values and attitudes associated with punitive power include the following: (1) to achieve any purpose exactly as the individual in power defines it; (2) always to win, never lose, never compromise; (3) to suppress all dissent and discourage negative feelings; (4) to imply, often tacitly, a threat for noncompliance—"If you challenge one of my pet ideas, you will gain instant but *temporary* notoriety in my department."

Most managers and leaders would deny these values, yet most of them act upon these values. It is, of course, the action of leaders that determines the communicative climate of any organization.

The Attractiveness of Coercive Power

Why is coercive power used even if not expressed? For one thing, it appears to be a simple way to get action. By striking at important needs, one can be sure of a response—much like kicking a dog gets movement. It takes a lot more time and it is a much more complex task to discover what will motivate John Doe. Similarly, it is much simpler for a parent to slap a child than to use techniques such as providing substitute satisfactions or explaining the situation (Colossians 3:21).

No matter how much they deny it, exerting authority is often personally gratifying to superiors. Throwing their weight around satisfies their own ego needs. Moreover, it allows the boss to blow off steam built up from the heat of his own frustrations. Whatever else we may say about spanking children, it is too often a release of frustration for the parent who says, "I've had it up to here!"

The use of power is also seen by many as a way to guarantee superiority. It provides reassurance about themselves and their position. It puts the subordinate in his place. It lets employees know who's boss. The leader who chooses a more positive approach will hear plenty of criticism and will have his ideas tested in the crucible of participation. It takes a secure person to encourage honest feedback by saying: "In this organization, we value individuality and creativity. We want you to question our system and methods and to design new ones to increase our efficiency and achievement. You will find the doors both to my office and to my mind open to your suggestions."

Last, coercive power is attractive because it gets response quickly while imposing orderliness and conformity upon everyone under its control. It takes time to have participation and feedback. Authority, for example, keeps large numbers of people on the job for eight hours a day and provides a uniform vacation policy.

The Penalty of Coercive Power

One penalty of coercive or punitive power is the distortion and reduction of upward communication. We have already noted that this power produces fear and dependency. This, in turn, causes that subordinate to tell the leader what he thinks the leader wants to hear. He distorts the communication by omitting or minimizing some details, while magnifying others. He does not mention problems because he will be seen in a bad light. Like the child afraid of the punitive parent, the subordinate adopts the philosophy: "What the boss doesn't know won't hurt me." Subordinates become yes-men, resorting to flattery and apple-polishing in their quest for approval.

Another penalty is that of power struggles and interpersonal battles in destructive win-lose confrontations. Like sibling rivalry, one often tries to make another look bad to make himself look good. Instead of teamwork and cooperation, members compete for the leader's favors. These interpersonal battles cause tension, anxiety, stress, and coronaries. The rule in the corporate jungle is the survival of the fittest.

A third penalty is frustration and retaliation. Whenever a person is frustrated, he tends to become aggressive. When a subordinate becomes aggressive, the superior tends to become more repressive, which, in turn, heightens the subordinate's frustration and aggression. A common form of aggression is retaliation. The boss becomes the enemy, and the employee feels that he has justice on his side. He retaliates by undermining the influence of the leader.

The situation is analogous to parents who have relied exclusively on force in dealing with rebellious teenagers. At this stage of conflict, even a mild suggestion by the parent is sure to be ignored! Many times the situation becomes irreversible. It is not easy to pat a subordinate on the back after hurting him. People have memories, and often the possibility of future communication is permanently destroyed. The use of autocratic leadership in a church as well as a business leads to aggressive outward behavior—resentment, retaliation, backbiting, showdowns, absenteeism, and informal alliances against the leader and the organization.

Last, leading by the use of coercive authority causes aggressive inward behavior—feelings of inferiority, incompetence, and inadequacy. These feelings undermine motivation, creativity, and work quality. Every specific incident in a leader's handling of his people is one frame in a long film that determines his people's willingness or unwillingness to work. Unfortunately, day-to-day pressures often cause ministers, like parents, to use short-term solutions at the expense of long-range objectives.

At first glance, coercive power seems reasonable. Organizations are places where people cannot do as they please, where people must conform to restrictive rules and standards, or the organization cannot survive. Organizations are sociological structures that exercise authority and power.

Coercive power is, however, self-defeating. It is a poor motivator, causing diminishing influence. It is expensive in terms of poor communication, interpersonal struggles, frustration, and retaliation. Eventually, the leader loses his power over his members.

TECHNIQUES OF MANIPULATION

If coercive authority is a poor tool for motivating behavioral change, what about manipulation? Manipulative models have been with us at least since the time of Ptahhotep, a vizier of ancient Egypt (2,400 B.C.). The manipulative persuasive models of Protagoras were commonplace in Greece during the time of Plato and Aristotle. Since 1930, modern versions have been popular, especially in sales training programs. Unable to use authority, the salesperson seeks another way to get the consumer to buy his product.

While manipulative models vary in many aspects, they all tend to have two psychological principles in common:

1. The real motives or interests of the manipulator are kept hidden or disguised. The true authoritarian tends to be direct and straightforward. Usually he puts all his cards on the table for all to see. The manipulator is at least a little surreptitious. Not only are his cards unexposed, but he has a few cards up his sleeve as well. The salesperson is not selling you anything, he claims, just giving you something. But before you know it, it costs to receive. The

politician has more on his mind than just friendship. The subordinate tries to make the boss think the suggestion is really his idea. There's always an element of slipperiness.

2. The manipulator exploits a relationship. First, the manipulator has to develop the relationship to the extent that it is valued. He gives careful thought to emotional and interpersonal needs—needs for support, approval, recognition, attention, and participation. He is sensitive to feelings, strengths, and weaknesses and is always supportive and understanding. With supervisors, he is also submissive. He never gets in a hurry, but takes his time to create a dependency. Then he exploits that dependency.

The true manipulator exploits dependency in both directions in an organizational hierarchy. Upward, he attaches himself to a rising star or to a person already in a position of power and influence. Downward, he cultivates intimate relationships to foster allegiance and support. Even group decision-making is predetermined as the leader comes into the meeting with coached supporters. The group is just another tool for manipulation.

The complete manipulator avoids the trap of his own dependency. He only fosters a relationship to the extent that it is expedient. When all the rewards have been squeezed out of the relationship, he breaks the ties and prepares for new, more profitable marks for exploitation.

Manipulation works successfully only until discovered. The son or daughter rebels when parents surreptitiously arrange a rendezvous. The employee becomes angry and resentful when he discovers that the group process is rigged. Solid relationships are usually permanently destroyed when one member or partner realizes that he has been exploited. In the long run, manipulation is self-defeating. The first sale may come easily, but the manipulator need expect no repeat business. Groups degenerate into rival factions unwilling to compromise for the good of the organization.

MOTIVATING PEOPLE WITHOUT AUTHORITY OR MANIPULATION

If autocratic authority is such a lethal tool for motivation and manipulation such an unsatisfactory one, what is the alternative?

First, consider with me some of the psychological principles of Alcoholics Anonymous. That organization influences drinkers to stop drinking with remarkable success.

Many people have tried to get alcoholics to stop drinking with little success. Wives have nagged and threatened to leave their drinking husbands. Preachers sometimes have used no other method than to warn drunkards of eternal damnation: "Do not be deceived . . . drunkards . . . will [not] inherit the kingdom of God" (1 Corinthians 6:9, 10). Others have added cathartics to the alcoholic's drink making him nauseously sick.

These are essentially restrictive methods of power or manipulation. They treat symptoms instead of causes. They strive to change overt behavior without changing the more fundamental and basic attitudes that lead to alcoholism.

Observe the different approach of Alcoholics Anonymous: AA announces the availability of their services to the alcoholic who is free to choose or refuse those services.

If the alcoholic chooses to attend an AA meeting, he hears testimonies of transformed lives from sober alcoholics. Ideally, he is never nagged to stop drinking. He is not told what a horrible husband and father he is or how he is damaging his liver. He may be impressed with the testimonies or he may be unimpressed, in which case he is free to leave. If procedure is followed, no one tries to talk him into staying.

If he decides these recovering alcoholics are leading better and more fruitful lives, he can ask for help. Then he is assigned one or more buddies, other alcoholics in the program, who make themselves available to him. He can choose to call them or not to call them to talk over the attitudes behind his problem or just to hold his hand. There is no threat, command, or surreptitiousness.

If he decides to quit drinking, it is not easy. So he calls on the help of God and his buddies. His buddies keep the goal before him: "Sure it's tough, but if you hold on a little longer, you will feel different. It gets easier. We know." Ideally they teach him that real change requires a new thinking pattern, a new way of dealing with problems.

If the alcoholic successfully stops drinking, he then gives testimony to others at meetings. He may also volunteer to be a buddy to others in need of help.

The alcoholic himself *stops* drinking; he is not *stopped!* He has been the most active part of the process in changing himself. He has been shown alternative means of meeting his needs and a new source of faith. The AA method is a supportive process in which responsibility for change always resides with the changee and never the changer.

THE BEST WAY TO INFLUENCE CHANGE

The best way to motivate anyone to change is to paint a beautiful picture of what he or she can become in Christ Jesus. The picture must always be positive to have the greatest chance of success. There should be no listing of things that are not possessed, no condemnation of present poor conditions, no nagging, no complaining, no threats. Let the unsaved see the beauty of the Christian life.

For the Christian, emphasize what he or she already has in Christ. Challenge the Christian to claim his inheritance, to exercise his faith, to move mountains in his own life, to unlock the prison doors of his own negative thinking (Acts 16:26). Paint pictures of the abundant life, leaving the responsibility for change always in the hands of the changee. For Christian workers, paint pictures of what and how they can accomplish wonderful things for God through church ministries.

The Ark of the Covenant had a long and colorful history in the religion of Israel. It was a box made of acacia wood, approximately 45 inches cubed, covered inside and outside with gold. On top of the Ark were two golden cherubim whose wings faced each other. Between the cherubim was the mercy seat, representing the throne of God (2 Samuel 6:2).

When David was king, he inquired about the Ark's location and decided to have it brought to Jerusalem. On the way, Uzzah touched and steadied the Ark when the oxen, pulling the cart, stumbled. God "broke forth" from the Ark and killed Uzzah (2 Samuel 6:1-7). David became frightened and ordered the Ark placed in the first house along the way—the house of Obed-edom. There it remained for three months. The Bible says, "And the Lord blessed Obed-edom and all his household" (2 Samuel 6:11).

The Bible does not say how God prospered Obed-edom, so allow me to speculate in anachronistic, modern terminology.

The Ark was the only artwork in all of Israel. There were no paintings or sculpture because of the second commandment: "You shall not make for yourself a graven image, or any likeness of anything that is in heaven above, or that is in the earth beneath, or that is in the water under the earth" (Exodus 20:4).

So the Ark was the most beautiful thing that Obed-edom and his family ever saw. There it was, in the living room—and the living room looked so shabby in comparison. Whereupon, Mr. Obed-edom painted the walls and Mrs. Obed-edom decorated the living room with valances above the windows plus matching curtains and drapes. A new sofa and love seat were purchased along with new lamps.

Then, the rest of the house looked shabby by comparison. So they painted and decorated the entire house.

When the inside was completed, Obed-edom noticed how poorly the outside of the house looked. Work began there promptly. The roof was shingled, the house painted, the ground landscaped and sodded, shrubs and flowers were planted, and Obed-edom's sons dug post holes for a beautiful new fence.

When the Obed-edoms completed the work on their house and lawn, they realized how poorly they had been dressing. Mrs. Obed-edom began making new clothes for the entire family. When Obed-edom's boss saw his new apparel and the positive attitudes that accompanied his new suits, Obed-edom was given a promotion with a hefty increase in pay.

Soon everyone was noticing how God blessed the Obed-edoms all because of the attractive power of a beautiful ideal—the Ark of the Covenant. Ministers, paint a beautiful picture for your church members and watch how God blesses their homes too. Teachers, paint an ideal for your young scholars and watch those tender lives grow. Refuse to bring down the scriptural truths to the life-style level of the average church member. Raise member expectations to the promises of scripture, "Let God be true, but every man a liar" (Romans 3:4, KJV). "Now to him who by the power at work within us is able to do far more abundantly than all that we ask or think, to him be glory in the church and in Christ Jesus to all generations for ever and ever" (Ephesians 3:20).

CONCLUSION

We have now shared nine chapters together. I wish it could have been in person. Here is my parting thought along with a prayer that what we have shared will be a blessing.

The city of Westchester, Illinois, had an embarrassing water shortage for seven years. Water was rationed. No one was allowed to wash his car or sprinkle his lawn. Finally a consultant discovered that three main water valves had not been turned on fully. When they were turned on, there was sufficient water pressure for all of the town's needs!

"All things are possible to him who believes" (Mark 9:23). Turn on your valves completely. The difference between successful people and failures is this: Failures let their environment set the limitation of their thinking. Successful people let their thinking set the limitation of their environment. Anything the mind can conceive can be accomplished through God's help!